PRAISE FOR
BLACK & GOLD

"Cadet X knocked this one out of the park! He always had big dreams and in this book he shares how he turned his dreams into a reality."
—*Cadet Y*

"This book hits real financial issues that face military members: real estate, retirement savings, and stock investing. If only I read this when I was a cadet, I wouldn't have blown my entire Cow Loan on buying that brand new Camaro."
—*Army Captain*

"I'm honestly surprised that Cadet X made it this far. I really thought he was going to get separated from West Point as a cadet, but somehow, he made it through and graduated. If I was the on his Reg. Board, I would have seperated him."
—*A former USMA Tactical Officer*

"I'm ashamed to say that I read this book. Unfortunately, it is much better than any books published by my fellow Naval Academy grads. There are great lessons in here for any service academy graduate. Well done West Point."
—*USNA Graduate*

Published by Black & Gold LLC.

First Paperback Edition
Version 1.00 published on December 4th, 2021
Printed in the United States

ISBN: 978-1-7353468-3-0

Library of Congress Cataloging Information available upon request.

For more information email TheCadetX@gmail.com

For my Mentors,

When I reported to West Point as a New Cadet, I knew nothing. Now, I know a little more and for much of it I have you to thank.

I am truly grateful for you.

BLACK &GOLD

AN OFFICER'S JOURNEY FROM WEST POINT TO MILLIONAIRE

CONTENTS

PREFACE	RULES OF ENGAGEMENT	11
PLEBE YEAR:	NET WORTH	13
YUCK YEAR:	PURE FUCKING MAGIC	21
COW YEAR:	INVESTMENTS	29
FIRSTIE YEAR:	GOALS	39
2002-2003	BUDGETS	45
2003-2004	FAMILY	55
2004-2005	THRIFT SAVINGS PLAN	61
2005-2006	CREDIT	69
2006-2007	RISK	75
2007-2008	BEAR MARKETS	85
2008-2009	PAY YOURSELF FIRST	91
2009-2010	INVESTMENT LIFECYCLES	97
2010-2011	DIVORCE	109
2011-2012	FIRST HOME	115
2012-2013	STARTUPS	125
2013-2014	STOCKS	135
2014-2015	RENTAL PROPERTIES	147
2015-2016	MARRIAGE	155
2016-2017	SIDE HUSTLES	163
2017-2018	ADVANCED TRADING	171
2018-2019	CRYPTO	197
2019-2020	CHILDREN	209
2020-2021	RETIREMENT	217
2021-2022	RETREAT	227

RULES OF ENGAGEMENT

This book is for entertainment purposes only. This book is not financial or legal advice. Before you make important financial, legal, or other life changing decisions, you should first do your own research and due diligence. Consult with a financial advisor, attorney, certified public accountant, or other professional before making decisions that can destroy your life.

I've changed many of the events and stories in this book to protect the privacy of my friends, family, coworkers, and myself. Any similarities to real people are coincidental.

My stories and opinions about companies, products, stocks, real estate, or other investments are examples and do not constitute an endorsement or financial advice. I may, or may not, have a financial interest in any of the stocks, products, or other assets that I talk about.

I've tried my best to present financial and regulatory information as accurately as possible given the information I had available at the time of publication. Still, I frequently make mistakes and I am sure that I've made many mistakes throughout this book. Furthermore, over time, the markets change, policies and laws change, and my opinions change. Please do not treat anything in this book as fact. This is yet another reason why you should do your own research and due diligence before making financial decisions.

Finally, my opinions are my own and do not represent the Department of Defense, Department of the Army, United States Military Academy, or any other organization.

PLEBE YEAR
NET WORTH

My parents and I sat in the bleachers of Michie Stadium. Sitting around us were about 50 other incoming West Point new cadets and their parents. My dad sat to my left and my mother sat to my right.

On the floor in between my feet, I had a JanSport backpack with a pair of black leather boots tied to the carrying handle. Inside the backpack, I had two changes of clothes, toiletries, a check book, and $100 in cash that my parents gave me. The check book was linked to my bank account, which had my life's savings—about $400—the product of working a part-time job at RadioShack during my senior year of high school.

In front of the bleachers, on the football field sideline, an Army officer provided a short information brief. He told our parents about the shuttle schedule and when they would be able to contact us again. At the end of the brief, he gave us 60 seconds to say goodbye to our parents.

In less than a minute, I gave my mom and dad hugs, I promised to write them letters as soon as I could, and I told them that I loved them. Other parents around us were crying and grasping their sons and daughters. They gripped their children and tried to make 60 seconds last longer than a minute.

"Just remember," my dad said as I picked up my backpack and boots, "Always have a sense of humor."

"I will Dad. I'll talk to you guys soon. I love you."

I put my backpack on and walked down the bleacher stairs. I joined the line of new cadets and we proceeded to walk across the football field to the row of buses that waited for us on the other side of the stadium. As I crossed the 50-yard line, I turned and waved goodbye to my mom and dad one more time. That morning, I started cadet basic training at the United States Military Academy at West Point.

That was over 20 years ago but it is still a vivid memory. That morning was the start of an incredible journey.

It would be impossible for me to explain all the ways that West Point has changed the trajectory of my life. Through my experience at West Point, and subsequent career as an Army officer, I have grown by leaps and bounds—professionally, academically, spiritually, and financially.

By most of society's measures, I've lived a remarkably successful life. I have a bachelor's degree from West Point and a master's degree from Vanderbilt. I served in the Army for 20 years and achieved the rank of lieutenant colonel. I am retired now and am preparing to start a civilian career, but my salary before retirement, including base pay and housing allowance, was about $150,000 a year. My wife is also a professional and makes about the same amount. Our assets include two rental properties with about $425,000 in equity, $275,000 in brokerage accounts, $100,000 in savings, $350,000 in my IRA, $200,000 in my TSP, $300,000 in my wife's retirement accounts, $50,000 in cryptocurrencies, plus another $75,000 in other assets, for a total combined net worth of about $1.7 million. Additionally, I have a full pension that I estimate to be worth about $2.5 million. My wife and I also own multiple businesses and a nonprofit organization.

Best of all, I have a beautiful family that I love and cherish. In addition to an intelligent and beautiful wife, I also have a beautiful daughter that bring me immense happiness and joy.

I'm not a smart guy. I've made a lot of mistakes as a cadet, in my career, in my relationships, and in my finances. Yet, for every mistake I've made, I've tried to learn from it and not repeat it. So far, that strategy has worked out well for me.

Although my financial growth is not the most important part of my journey, it is the part of the journey that is the primary subject of this book.

I wrote this book for cadets and young military officers for two reasons. The first reason why I wrote this book is because I grew up in a modest lower-middle-class family. My parents taught me the value of hard work, but they did not teach me about personal financial management or investment strategies. Personal financial management is a key pillar of living a rewarding life and I hope that my lessons can help other young officers from similar disadvantaged communities.

Before I go on, I need to give you the disclaimer. This book is not financial advice. It is merely my story and how I approach life. I'm not an expert. I'm not a lawyer, certified public accountant, financial advisor, doctor, or spiritual leader. The topics I talk about in this book can change your life, for better or worse. One person that follows my lead may become a millionaire, but someone else who follows my path may end up in bankruptcy. The lessons I'm going to share in this book have helped me, but I don't make any promises that they will do the same for you. To be financially successful, you will need to learn your own lessons, but I hope that my example can accelerate your learning curve.

The second reason why I wrote this book is because many young officers get out of the Army as soon as they can. They think that they can make more money as a civilian, but that is not always the case. I hope that my story can show you that you can have an extremely rewarding 20-year military career and become financially independent in the process.

It's important to hear other people's financial stories, especially from people that have similar experiences and career paths as yourself. Unfortunately, those stories are few and far between.

Throughout school and my early career, I always had senior officers tell me, "Save in your TSP and Roth IRA," but I can't remember a single time where an officer ever shared their own financial numbers. You would think that in a profession where we all know how much each other make, that talking about money would be less taboo, but it's not. Whether people are ashamed or afraid of bragging, people just don't talk about their wealth. As a result, I think that cadets and young officers are missing out on valuable lessons that could help them improve their financial acumen.

A lot has changed since I entered West Point in the late 1990s. As a new cadet, I did not have a debit card, credit card, cell phone, brokerage account, or cash apps. In the 90s, cash, checks, and credit cards were still the main way that people spent or exchanged money. Smart phones were still nearly a decade away. Although technology and the world we live in has changed, many of the fundamental principles that have helped me become financially successful still apply today. One of those principals is net worth.

Throughout my career, I've calculated my net worth at least once per year. In my opinion, net worth is a strong indicator of your financial freedom, more so than your salary. I always recommend young officers to do the same. Net worth is the sum of your assets (savings, retirement, car value, home value, etc.) minus liabilities (credit card debts, loan balances, mortgage balances, etc.). The first step in a journey begins with knowing where you are. If you have not done so already, take a moment and calculate your net worth.

Today, my wife and I are millionaires as measured by our net worth. The journey to get here started when I was a young cadet with $500 to my name.

Depending on who you talk to, a million dollars may or may not be a lot of money. Where I'm from, a million dollars is a lot of money!

Today, after spending decades in school and serving my country for 20 years, I am privileged. But that was not always the case. The neighborhood where I grew up, outside of Washington D.C., was predominantly middle and lower class. Most families, including my own, were hard working blue-collar workers. Growing up in a predominantly Black and Latino lower-income community, my family and the families of my friends just didn't have a lot of money.

There are a lot of different opinions on what income and wealth levels make up the different economic classes. I like to use this model, which is adapted from U.S. Census Bureau statistics.

U.S. Economic Classes

Income Group (% of US Households)	Household Income	Net Worth
Poor or near-poor (20%)	$20,000 or less	Less than $0
Lower-middle class (20%)	$20,000–$50,000	About $0
Middle class (40%)	$50,000–$120,000	$0–$500,000
Upper-middle class (15%)	$120,000–$260,000	$500,000–$2.5 million
Upper class (4%)	$260,000–$420,000	$2.5 million–$10 million
Top 1%	$420,000 and up	$10 million and up

U.S. Economic Classes. Reprinted with permission from *Alpha Couples: Build a Powerful Marriage Like a Boss* (2020), by Robert Solano and Zaira Solano.

To put these numbers in context, the average new lieutenant in the Army earns about $60,000 per year when you include housing allowance, which is just barely at the start of middle class. In contrast, a senior lieutenant colonel at twenty years of service earns about $150,000 per year. With a salary above $120,000 and a net worth of between $500,000 and $2.5 million, most military officers can expect to be in upper-middle class or upper class after a 20-year career.

The truth is that a million dollars today does not have the same value that a million dollars had 20 years ago. A million dollars of net worth can provide you some financial stability, but maybe not enough that you would immediately quit your job. Some experts say that the new millionaire status should start at net worth of three million which is just above the start of the upper class. Still, a net worth of a million dollars is enough to live relatively comfortably. More so, it is an amount that allows most people to make substantial investment decisions, take occasional risks, and work in jobs that are professionally fulfilling rather than working in jobs out of immediate necessity.

I suspect that some of my more intelligent and fiscally prudent peers have saved and accumulated much more wealth than me. At the same time though, I know that many of my peers have saved much less. If you learn from my story, and avoid my mistakes, I hope that you will be in the first category and not the latter.

My story is not an overnight-rags-to-riches story. I didn't invest in a moonshot startup and suddenly become a millionaire, nor did I bet all my chips on a risky asset like Bitcoin and quadruple my net worth over night. Instead, my story is one of sporadic, small, and diversified investments throughout 20 years. It is also a story about the many mistakes and missed opportunities along the way. I hope to show you that a million dollars is a very achievable net worth for most young professionals.

Regardless of if you think that a million dollars is a lot or not, the reality is that you need to save and invest one million dollars before you can get to three million, ten million, or more. Personally, I have my long-term goal set at 6.5 million, which I believe is the amount I need to live comfortably to 100 years old. And yes, I believe that medical advancements in the next few decades, combined with a healthy lifestyle, will allow me to live comfortably to 100 years old. This book is only the first phase of me achieving that goal. Whatever your net worth goal, I hope that my lessons can help you.

The road to financial freedom is a journey. I've been on the journey for over 20 years and still, almost every day, I hear a concept or idea that reminds me just how little I know. I still feel like a new cadet sometimes, grasping to understand the deep and complex world of finances. In many ways, my journey as an adult, as an officer, and as a millionaire began when I crossed that 50-yeard line at Michie Stadium and that journey is still continuing.

LET'S RECAP

Investing is a continuous learning process. The techniques that work for one person may not work for you. You will need to learn what works for you.

Before making life changing financial decisions, you should do your own research and consult with a financial or legal professional if required.

Your net worth is the sum of your assets minus liabilities. You should calculate your net worth periodically to measure your progress in achieving financial freedom.

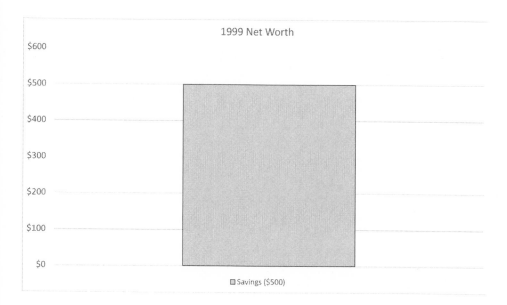

This book is organized by years. At the end of each chapter, I share my approximate net worth for that year in my life. Plebe year, my net worth was about $500.

YUCK YEAR
PURE FUCKING MAGIC

"P-F-M," the Army captain said as he pointed to each of the letters on the chalk board, "It's pure effing magic. You don't need to understand it. All you need to know is that it's magic. You put your money aside, forget about it, and then it just starts magically growing."

The personal financial management (PFM) class was a mandatory 90-minute lecture during West Point's annual one-week intersession period. For one week, we took a break from academic work and instead focused on military drills, prevention of sexual harassment training, and other important, but nonacademic related topics. For this session, an Army Reserves Officer was serving his annual two-weeks of drill by teaching us about personal finances. From that lecture, there are three things that I remember: 1) PFM, 2) something about a Roth IRA, and 3) the Black instructor.

That short class was the first time in my entire life that I ever had a Black teacher. I honestly never really noticed that all of my teachers since kindergarten had been White, and seeing my first Black instructor at West Point was incredibly surprising.

I grew up near Washington D.C. My father was a construction worker and my mom was a secretary. Although they did not make a lot of money, they worked extra hard to send me to private school for elementary and high school. In private school my teachers were always White. The only non-Caucasian teachers were an occasional Latina Spanish language teacher.

Throughout my entire life, I had become so conditioned to the lack of diversity in education that I never seriously questioned it. As a Black Latino cadet, it was rewarding to finally see a teacher that looked like me. The fact that this Black instructor was also teaching us how to become rich was equally surprising.

The instructor talked to us about a special type of account called a Roth IRA. While growing up, my parents never discussed retirement savings with me. I always believed that "the only things certain in life are death and taxes," but apparently the Roth IRA was some kind of exception. After an initial deposit, the Roth IRA was generally tax-free or tax exempt.

Not only did the Roth IRA have tax advantages, but it also had something called compounding interest, which the instructor referred to as pure fucking magic, PFM. I never imagined that I would be able to save over $100,000, but the instructor provided a few examples of how that was actually possible with compounding interest.

In a simple math example, the instructor showed how compounding interest could repeatedly double an account balance every 10 years so that an initial investment of $10,000 at 20 years old could turn into $160,000 by the time you were 60 years old—$10,000 at 20 years old, $20,000 at 30, $40,000 at 40, $80,000 at 50, and $160,000 at 60 years old.

When I said goodbye to my father at Michie Stadium, he was about 60 years old. My parents had some money saved up for retirement, but definitely not $160,000. The idea that a small investment as a cadet could turn into, what I perceived to be, a life changing amount of money, fascinated me. Unfortunately, at the time I only had about $300 in my bank account.

The following week, I called Charles Schwab to see if I could open up a Roth IRA with my $300. The man on the other line nearly laughed at me when he told me that the minimum required to open an account was $2,500. Today, most brokerages will allow investors to start an IRA with $0, but 20 years ago, that was not the case.

My Yuck year, I was only making about $200 a month. After paying my phone bill and paying for an occasional pizza from Schade's, saving up $2,500 was out of the question. Without any options, I put the idea aside.

A few months later, my beloved grandmother passed away—*rest in peace Nanny*. As a departing gift, she left each of her eight grandchildren an inheritance. Each of us received a whopping $2,000.

As a Yuck, $2,000 was a huge sum of money. I was tempted to spend it on something fun. At the time, I had an upcoming 4-day weekend pass for Columbus Day. I considered getting a nice hotel room in New York City and then taking my girlfriend out to dinner and dancing. As a cadet on lockdown in the barracks most of the time, it would have been nice to go out to a bar in the city like a normal college kid and sleep in the same bed with my girlfriend. I was tempted, but I really wanted to open up a Roth IRA account.

When the weekend came, instead of taking my girlfriend to the city, I borrowed a car from a Firstie and drove to the nearest Charles Schwab office, which was about 45 minutes away. I walked in with my $2,000 plus another $500 that I managed to save and requested to open a Roth IRA.

I vaguely remember the associate at Schwab explain to me that I could use my Roth IRA to invest in mutual funds or stocks. I didn't know a lot about stocks, but I knew even less about mutual funds. My limited knowledge about stocks was from my high school AP Economics teacher.

In economics class, our teacher introduced us to micro and macroeconomics, the law of supply and demand, and the stock market. General Electric was his favorite company and he frequently used it as an example whether talking about the supply and demand of refrigerators or the stock market.

My teacher was an older man and taught high school as a second career after he retired from a corporate career at General Electric. He frequently talked about how much money he made from GE stock.

When it came time to invest my inheritance, which was now in my Roth IRA, I remembered my high school teacher. I used half of my big inheritance to buy General Electric stock (ticker symbol GE). The other half I used to buy stock in Lockheed Martin (ticker symbol LMT).

My reason for selecting Lockheed was very calculated. In high school, I played the MS-DOS based video game, *Apache*. It was my first introduction to the badass AH-64 helicopter. I thought that Lockheed made the Apache so I believed that Lockheed would be an awesome stock to own.

In actuality, I didn't know jack shit about either company. Lockheed didn't make the Apache, Boeing did. Lockheed only made some of the Apache's avionics equipment, but I didn't know that at the time because I didn't do any due diligence.

When I invested in the companies, GE stock traded for about $49.60 per share and LMT traded for about $21.80. With my newly created Roth IRA, I bought 20 shares of GE and 40 shares of LMT. Now that I had my first investment, all I had to do was wait for the Pure Fucking Magic.

When I think about PFM, I like to imagine a magic penny.

Answer this question: Imagine a magic penny that doubles in quantity every day for 31 days. So that the second day it would be 2 cents, the third day it would be 4 cents, fourth day 8 cents, and so on for 31 days.

If I gave you a choice, would you rather take the magic penny or ten thousand dollars?

Most people instinctively believe that ten thousand dollars is worth more than the penny would be after 31 days. Since you are smarter than me, you would probably realize that this is a trick question.

The next question is: How much do you think the pile of magic pennies would be worth after 31 days?

Ten thousand dollars, which is one million pennies? A hundred thousand dollars? One million dollars?

After 31 days, the pile of pennies would be worth significantly more than a million dollars. If you calculate it out, the pile of magic pennies would be worth $10,737,418.24. That's a lot of freaking pennies!

A single penny, compounding daily at a 100% interest rate, can quickly turn into ten million dollars. That is the power of compounding interest.

Now, imagine if that penny continued to double every day for an entire year.

It would be impossible for the penny to double for 365 days because by February you would have all of the U.S. currency in circulation—all $1.2 trillion dollars of it!

If your magic penny continued compounding, by March your pile of pennies would weigh more than the entire Earth.

We can't all be lucky enough to find a magic penny that compounds daily at 100% interest, but smaller interest rates have magical power too. For example, an investment with an annual interest rate of 7.2% will double every 10 years. In comparison, the NASDAQ, which is a collection of big tech stocks like Google, Microsoft, and Intel, averaged 14.4% interest over the past ten years. At 14.4% interest rate, an investment doubles every 5 years.

As a 19-year-old cadet, if I were lucky enough to get a 7.2% interest rate on my $2,000 investment, I would have had $4,000 at 29 years old, $8,000 at 39, $16,000 at 49, $32,000 at 59, and $64,000 at 69. Turning $2,000 into $64,000 is definitely magic.

The challenge is that to take advantage of PFM and compounding interest, you need to accept delayed gratification. As a horny 19-year-old cadet, it was difficult to sacrifice a romantic weekend in New York City with my girlfriend in order to open up a Roth IRA, but I somehow knew that sacrificing that one weekend as a cadet would get me laid later in life.

It's important to note that the $64,000 estimate was only based on an initial investment of $2,000. If you double, triple, or quadruple that number, the return on investment (ROI) later in life increases accordingly.

The key to PFM is time. Interest rates need time to compound. At first, the growth rate seems small, but overtime initial investments will grow exponentially. To highlight this, let's look at the magic penny. The first 6 days of the month, the magic penny would grow to a humble $1.28.

Now, let's fast forward to the end of the month. On day 25, the magic penny is only worth $167,000. But less than six days later, on day 31, it is worth over $10 million. The first six days, the investment grows by about one dollar. The last six days, the investment grows by nine million dollars—that is the power of compounding interest.

The same is true for investments. If I were lucky enough to get a 7.2% interest rate, my IRA would only grow by $2,000 from ages 19 to 29. However, that same investment would grow by $32,000 from the ages of 59 to 69.

When it comes to compounding interest, you need to start investing early and you need to be patient. If you start early, exponential returns come later in life. For compounding interest, investing early is the key, even if you don't know what you are doing.

When I bought my GE and LMT stock, I didn't really understand the stock market or Roth IRAs, but I followed the advice from the Nike commercials—"Just Do It!"

Too many cadets and lieutenants sit on the sidelines because they don't understand Roth IRAs, Thrift Savings Plans, mutual funds, stocks, or taxes. For every year that they wait, they lose opportunities for compounding interest. I've been investing for over 20 years, and there is still a lot I don't understand, but I still invest anyway. For me, "learning as you go" has always been a better strategy than "learning before you go." If a cadet asks me for investment advice, my response is simple, "Just do it!"

If I had to give advice to a normal civilian college student, my advice would probably be different. Civilian students need to pay for college, their living expenses, and worry about finding a job after college. Most cadets don't have those same worries.

As a cadet or young officer, you are fortunate that you have college paid for and a job waiting for you. You are in a much better position to begin investing early in life than your civilian counterparts and this time advantage is a magic multiplier.

7.2% is a unique number because that is the interest rate required to double an investment every 10 years. If you are smart though, you can outperform that. As an example, the average interest rate of return for the S&P 500 (500 large companies in the stock market) is about 9.2%, which would double an investment about every 8 years. The difference between a 7.2% interest rate compared to a 9.2% interest rate, could be the difference between retiring at 65 years old or retiring at 55 years old with the same amount of wealth. With compounding interest, small changes in interest rate have huge impacts over time.

With stocks, the way I measure the equivalent interest rate is by taking the difference between the purchase price and sales price (or current price), and then dividing by the purchase price and time period.

As a field grade officer, I eventually sold my Lockheed and General Electric stock 16 years later. During that time, the stock price for Lockheed rose from $21.80 to $195—a 50% average annual rate of return. I sold my 40 shares at a $7,300 profit. After I sold LMT, I bought stock in Tesla (TSLA) at a cost basis of about $40 per share. When I sold half my TSLA stock five years later, I netted over $100,000 in profit. Best of all, since I invested it inside my Roth IRA, all my proceeds were tax exempt. Turning $1,000 into $100,000 in 20 years is definitely pure fucking magic!

With stocks, rates of returns are not guaranteed. In fact, all returns are unrealized until you sell the stock. I'll talk more about my stock market strategy later, but first I want to highlight an important lesson.

If the power of compounding interest is the first and most important lesson for financial freedom, the second most important lesson is that past performance does not guarantee future success.

I got lucky with Lockheed, and I had better strategy when I invested in Tesla, but what worked 10 or 20 years ago will probably not work in the future.

Remember that GE stock? The stock that my economics instructor raved about? The stock that made him so much money that he was set for life?

As a Yuck, I bought 20 shares at about $50 each for a total of $1000. When I sold the stock 15 years later, it was worth $25 per share. I lost half of my initial investment. I would have been better off using that money and taking my cadet girlfriend to New York City. 15 years later $500 would barely be enough to cover the cost of a nice dinner and a few cocktails.

In 1985, GE was $3 per share. In 1998, when I was in high school, it was $30. No wonder my economics instructor loved the stock. In 15 years, he probably increased his wealth 10-fold. However, past performance does not guarantee future success and after GE peaked in 2000, it was all downhill from there.

Although I lost $500 on General Electric, the $7,300 I gained with Lockheed Martin certainly made up for my loss.

Throughout this book, I'll share similar success and failure stories. Each chapter generally follows my financial progression from West Point through my current position preparing for retirement. Along the way, I will share my personal experiences to highlight different aspects of personal financial management. There are certain topics that I won't cover because they have not happened in my life. For example, I've never traded the Foreign Exchange Market (Forex) nor have I ever hired a financial advisor service like First Command. Still, I think my experiences cover a broad range of financial situations and topics that are relevant to most cadets and junior officers.

When it comes to investing in stocks, real estate, businesses, or crypto I don't recommend that you try to imitate my strategy. What worked for me will probably not work for you. Instead, it is more important to understand the principles behind those strategies and why they succeeded or failed. You'll need to develop your own strategies.

LET'S RECAP

Compounding interest is pure fucking magic. Begin investing now, even if you don't fully understand everything, just do it.

Past performance does not guarantee future success.

Delayed gratification, especially early in your career, can lead to exponential wealth later in life.

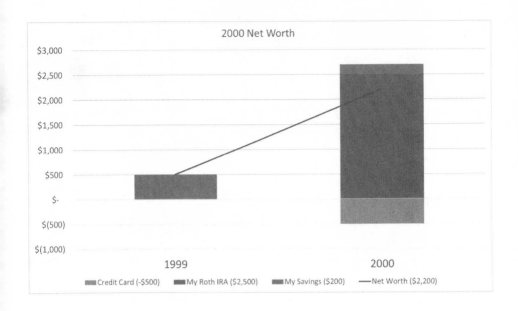

COW YEAR

INVESTMENTS

I broke up with my girlfriend the week before Spring Break. We previously planned to take a road trip together, but since we separated, I had to come up with some new plans. My roommate was equally without plans.

At Thursday night's dinner, we brainstormed Spring Break ideas. A classmate at our table mentioned that they were going to Jamaica. Jamaica sounded like a great idea to us! We returned to our room after dinner and bought two round trip tickets to Jamaica.

Spring Break was peak travel season and our flights departed in 36 hours. Although the tickets were ridiculously expensive, we were both Juniors and recently received our $25,000 Cow Loans. We were eager to spend it on a good time.

The Cow Loan is a lump sum, low interest rate loan, provided to all West Point cadets to helped them with upcoming graduation expenses, car purchases, and class rings. For my class, it was $25,000, at slightly less than 1% interest rate, repayable over a 5-year period. Today, the Cow Loan is about $35,000.

Saturday morning, my roommate and I took the train from Garrison to Grand Central and then caught a taxi to LaGuardia. A few hours later, we landed in Kingston.

When we arrived in Jamaica, I stopped at the ATM to withdraw some spending cash. I selected the largest amount of money from the withdrawal menu, $1600 Jamaican Dollars (JMD). When the receipt printed, it showed my balance as $1,036,476.24 JMD. Thanks to a favorable exchange rate, it was the first time in my life that I was a millionaire.

When we arrived in Jamaica, we didn't have a hotel or rental car reservations. The day before our last-minute trip, we frantically called different resorts around the island to try to book a hotel, but everywhere we called was sold out due to Spring Break. Although we didn't have any reservations, we thought that we had enough money to figure something out after we landed.

At the airport, we went to each of the rental car counters to try to get a car, but none would rent to us since we were under 25 years old. This was still before the age of smart phones and Wi-Fi, so our options were extremely limited. After begging all the rental car clerks, we were shit out of luck. We had no hotel, no car, and no plan.

We exited the airport and prepared to get a taxi, but we didn't even know where we would take the taxi to. As soon as we exited the airport terminal, taxi drivers, bell hops, and drug dealers swarmed on us. Everyone was trying to help us with our bags, offer us a ride somewhere, or sell us drugs and prostitutes. My dark skin helped me blended in with the locals, but my White blonde hair roommate wreaked of American money. Everyone wanted to sell him something.

A drug dealer approached us, "Whatcha wan? Blow? Ganja? Girls? I get you da best girls. Real tight pussy. They luv you long time, mon."

My roommate and I laughed and waved him off. We were not interested in catching a disease or jeopardizing our military careers. "Nah man. We're cool. We're just trying to find a rental car. You know where we can get one?"

The drug dealer thought for a moment and then replied, "Rental car? I gad yah mon. Come wid me. I take you to my uncle. He gad rental cars."

My roommate and I talked it over for a moment, figured we didn't have anything to lose, and then got in the car with a Jamaican drug dealer to go to his uncle's rental car spot—we were fucking idiots. When you get your Cow Loan, I hope that you don't do anything stupid like us. Have a plan.

With my Cow Loan, I made a lot of mistakes, but I also stumbled into a few really good decisions. Splurging on a last-minute Spring Break trip to Jamaica and then getting into a car with a drug dealer were bad decisions. While Spring Break in Jamaica is a great idea, the last minuteness and poor planning of our trip was where we went wrong.

As a wiser investor now, when I give Cow Loan advice to cadets, my advice is simple. In order of importance, I recommend: 1) max out your Roth IRA for the current and previous years, 2) buy a used car, 3) budget some money for graduation expenses like your ring, uniforms, bills, and class pistol—yes, get the pistol—and 4) go travel and see the world.

I strongly encourage cadets to max out their Roth IRA before they do anything else.

A Roth IRA is a type of Individual Retirement Account (IRA). Two other popular types of IRAs are the Traditional IRA and SIMPLE IRA. The SIMPLE IRA must be offered by an employer and since the Army offers the Thrift Savings Plan instead of the SIMPLE IRA or 401(k), you can ignore that type of IRA for now. The Thrift Savings Plan (TSP) is the military's retirement plan which is similar to civilian 401(k)s. I will talk more about the TSP in a later chapter, which leaves the two main types of IRAs, the Roth IRA and Traditional IRA.

Both IRA types are individually managed. Almost any taxpayer can create one of these IRA accounts with their financial institutions, like I did when I was a Yuck. Most financial institutions offer IRA accounts that are nearly identical to a brokerage account. Within most IRA accounts, you can invest in stocks, mutual funds, or exchange traded funds (ETFs). If you own stocks, you generally own a small share of a company. If you own mutual funds or ETFs, you own a collection of many different stocks, bonds, or other assets.

The key difference between a regular brokerage account and an IRA account is that the IRA account provides unique tax benefits. The main difference between the Roth and the Traditional IRA is the type of tax benefits.

In most circumstances, cadets and junior officers should invest in the Roth instead of the Traditional. To illustrate why this is, let's compare a regular brokerage account, Roth IRA, and Traditional IRA.

Let's assume that as a first lieutenant with four years' experience, you will earn $60,000 in taxable income per year and that your tax bracket is 20%. Let's also assume that you have $6,000 to spare which you want to invest. You are evaluating three different investment vehicles: a brokerage account, Traditional IRA, or Roth IRA.

To make the comparison simple, let's assume that with each account type, you could invest in the same mutual fund which you expect to earn an average annual return of 7.2% per year for 40 years. That rate will double your investment every decade. Therefore, if you invest $6,000 at 25 years old, it would be worth $96,000 at 65 years old.

For investing in a regular brokerage account, you also need to consider your annual taxes. To invest $6,000, you actually need to earn about $7,500. In our simple scenario, you would pay $1,500 in taxes on $7,500 earned which leaves you with $6,000 to invest after taxes. You would pay these taxes the year that you earned your income, at 25 years old.

When you withdraw your $96,000 40 years later, you will also pay a type of taxes called capital gains taxes. Capital gains taxes are also about 20%. So, if you invested in a regular brokerage account, you would pay $1,500 in taxes as a first lieutenant and then $19,200 in taxes as a 65-year-old.

For the next example, let's evaluate the benefits of the Traditional IRA. In a Traditional IRA, taxes are deferred until you withdraw your retirement savings. So, an initial investment of $6,000 would be tax exempt at 25 years old. A $6,000 investment will only cost you $6,000 and not $7,500.

Later, when you withdraw the funds at 65 years old, you would need to pay taxes as if it were your income. So, on the $96,000 in gains you would need to pay anywhere from 15 to 35% depending on your tax bracket. For this example, we will say that your future tax bracket is 25%. On $96,000, you would pay $24,000 in taxes.

In contrast, if you invested in a Roth IRA, you would pay your normal taxes as a first lieutenant ($1,500) and then future earnings are tax exempt. At 65 years old, you can withdraw all $96,000 tax free. It doesn't make a difference how much money you earn in a Roth IRA, you pay taxes on your income for the year that you contribute to the Roth IRA and you never pay taxes again (as long as you follow the IRA rules). You could do really well and make millions of dollars in your Roth IRA and all of it would be tax exempt.

If the math was confusing, this table should help clarify the differences.

IRA vs. Brokerage Comparison

	Brokerage	Traditional IRA	Roth IRA
Pre-Tax Earning	$7,500	$6,000	$7,500
Year 1 Taxes (20%)	$1,500	$0	$1,500
Initial Investment	$6,000	$6,000	$6,000
Balance after 40 years	$96,000	$96,000	$96,000
Year 40 Tax Rate	20%	25%	0%
Year 40 Taxes	$19,200	$24,000	$0
After Tax Profit	$76,800	$72,000	$96,000

There are a lot of simplifications in these comparison, but it should be clear that in this example the Roth IRA option pays much less taxes over the life of the investment.

Here is the best part though, the previous example was for a senior first lieutenant making $60,000 a year and paying about 20% of that in taxes. Cadets make substantially less than that. They usually pay 10% or less in taxes. Paying 10% in taxes as a cadet, to have an investment that will forever be tax exempt, is fucking amazing.

I plan to invest in my Roth accounts for as long as possible. The tax benefits of these accounts cannot be matched.

There are some technical limits to investing in a Roth or Traditional IRA. To begin, there is a limit for how much you can invest in your IRA each year. Currently the limit is $6,000 but it changes every few years.

The first day that you can invest in an IRA for a given year is January 1st of that year. The last day you can invest per year usually extends to the IRS tax filing deadline (around April 15th) of the following year. Therefore, a cadet that receives their Cow Loan in March 2022, can invest $6,000 in their Roth IRA for the current year (2022) and an additional $6,000 for the previous year (2021), for total single deposit of $12,000 into their IRA.

There is also a 10% penalty if you make withdrawals from your IRA before the age of 59 ½. If you withdraw from your Roth IRA before this age, you may also need to pay income tax. This age limit is why these are retirement accounts. There are some exceptions to the penalty. For example, you can make withdrawals for qualified education expenses or first-time home purchases. Generally though, most investors should avoid withdrawing from their retirement accounts before the age limit.

There are other IRA rules, but these are the basics. The deposit limits and minimum withdrawal age occasionally change, so you should read the IRS website to get the latest policies and tax codes. The annual limit is the most important number to know and you should check it annually. I recommend that most cadets and young officers try to invest up to this annual limit.

When I received my Cow Loan, I didn't max out my Roth IRA and I regret it now. Instead, I spent $3,000 on a trip to Jamaica, $3,100 on my class ring, $1,500 on my uniforms, $1,000 to pay off my credit card, $4,500 on a summer trip to Europe, $5,000 on a used car, and another few thousand on bullshit. When all my money was accounted for, I had $1,500 remaining which I put into my Roth

IRA and used to invest in an S&P 500 fund. I did not get the class pistol, which I regret, and now I have spent the past few years trying to find one.

Shortly after spring break, I started dating a Plebe—another bad decision. With about $1,000 of my Cow Loan, I planned to take my new girlfriend to New York City. I booked a hotel, made dinner reservations, and had the entire weekend planned.

Two days before my weekend pass, I got put on academic probation for having a D average in one of my classes. My pass was revoked. Frustrated by the policy, I decided to blow post and spend the weekend in the city anyway.

I hoped that by putting a few pillows under my green girl blanket that the officer in charge of quarters would mark me as present during Saturday night Taps checks. My plan failed and I had to report to my tactical officer after I returned on Sunday night. I received a disciplinary board for blowing post and a brief demotion to corporal.

My story was captured and distributed to my company in a disciplinary action summary involving the infamous pseudonym Cadet X.

It was an epic weekend and well worth the 25 hours of walking tours that I received as punishment.

If I made a few bad decisions as a Cow, the one good decision I made was buying a used car. My father had a two-year-old Ford Ranger pickup truck that he wanted to upgrade. Instead of trading it in, he offered to sell it to me at a discount. The value of the truck was about $13,000 but he offered to give it to me for $5,000.

I didn't want a pickup truck—I really wanted a Ford Mustang—but I could not pass up an $8,000 discount. I am incredibly grateful to my dad for that generous gift. I bought the truck from my dad during the summer after my Cow year and drove it back to West Point.

Ten years later, as a senior captain, I was still driving my Ford Ranger when the wheel nearly fell off. I was driving down the highway when the front axle broke. The wheel went sideways, and I lost steering control. Luckily, I was able to hobble the truck over to the shoulder and get it towed.

After I got the axel repaired, I continued to drive that truck for another three years. I didn't buy my first new car until I was a major, thirteen years after I bought the Ford Ranger from my dad. That decision, to buy a reliable used car as a cadet, saved me tens of thousands of dollars during my early career. If you are serious about building wealth, you should always buy a used or new car, preferably one that is highly rated and will retain its value for a long time. You should absolutely never, ever lease a car.

On the topic of cars, you will also need car insurance. Insurance options can be overwhelming, but the strategy that has helped me has been to always select the highest deductibles that I could afford. As a cadet and lieutenant, I usually selected a $500 deductible, meaning that if I got into an accident, I would need to pay $500 and insurance would cover the rest. Later on, as a captain, I increased this to $1,000. I've also usually turned down the extra features like rental car reimbursement and glass repair. This strategy has saved me a lot of money in the long run.

When it comes to insurance, it is also utterly important to get renters insurance before you get your class ring. I've known many cadets who have lost their ring during the course of Ring Weekend parties.

Renters insurance as a cadet is usually ridiculously cheap, usually less than $100 for the entire year, and can cover the cost of your ring or laptop if they get lost or stolen.

Buying a used car, instead of a new one, was a great investment decision. However, my best Cow Loan investment decision was taking the trip to Jamaica.

I wish that my roommate and I planned our trip ahead of time, but despite paying last-minute premiums on everything and having to get a rental car from a drug dealer, the trip was actually great!

Surprisingly, the drug dealer was legitimate. He took us to his uncle's rental car shop about 15 minutes from the airport and his uncle provided us a car at a reasonable rate. Before leaving the office, the drug dealer offered us drugs and prostitutes one more time, which we politely declined, and then we headed out on our journey to find a hotel.

We knew our classmates from Thursday night dinner were also arriving to Jamaica later that evening, so we headed to meet them at their hotel. The hotel was sold out, but after waiting in the lobby for a few hours, we got a room after someone cancelled. Over the next week, we had a great time partying, drinking Bob Marley shots, and exploring Jamaica. We went zip lining, hiked Ocho Rios, and went to a reggae concert with Shaggy as the headliner. At the time "Mr. Bombastic" was still popular and "It Wasn't Me" was topping the Billboard charts. It was amazing to see the most popular reggae artist in the world, in Jamaica, where reggae is king.

Later that summer, I used another portion of my Cow Loan to explore Paris, Barcelona, and London before I reported to an Advanced Individual Academic Development (AIAD) internship in the United Kingdom. It was my first time going to Europe and I will forever remember seeing the Eiffel Tower light show, seeing the Mona Lisa at the Louvre, eating tapas at an old Ernest Hemmingway hang out in Barcelona, and drinking pints of cider in London with a group of South Africans I befriended.

In all, those trips cost about $7,500, or one third of my loan. By far, they were the best investments I could have made with my Cow Loan. When I look back at my life over the past 25 years, the memories and experiences that I shared with friends and family are the highlights. Surpassing one million dollars in net worth was a huge personal achievement, but the memories of my world travels bring me more happiness and joy than the balance in my bank accounts. With every passing year, the memories from Jamaica, Europe, and the other 30 countries I've visited since, become stronger and more magical. Investments in experiences also have compounding interest.

LET'S RECAP

If I had to invest a Cow Loan today, I would 1) max out my Roth IRA for the current and previous years, 2) buy a used car, 3) budget some for graduation expenses, and 4) travel.

Travel and Spring Break excursions with friends are opportunities that cadets should take advantage off. Experiences are also an investment.

Planning ahead and budgeting your Cow Loan can prevent you from making poor financial decisions.

INVESTMENTS

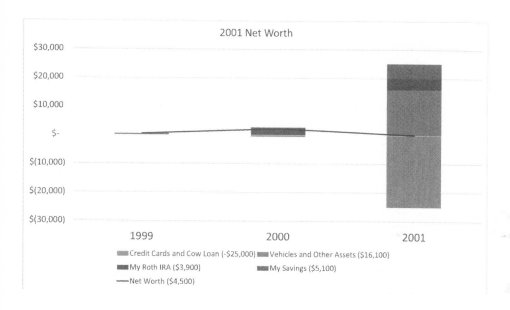

2001 Net Worth

Credit Cards and Cow Loan (-$25,000)   Vehicles and Other Assets ($16,100)
My Roth IRA ($3,900)   My Savings ($5,100)
Net Worth ($4,500)

FIRSTIE YEAR GOALS

When I was a First Class cadet at West Point, I received an email from brigade headquarters requesting volunteers to attend a dinner cruise with West Point alumni.

Old Grads love hanging out with cadets, and volunteer requests for social events, dinner parties, and tours were common. I had attended boat cruises on the Hudson a couple of times. Usually, they were one of those 50 to 100 passenger double decker booze cruise boats that travelled up and down the river for two or three hours. Occasionally, cadet companies rented them for end-of-year parties.

This request was for a Wednesday night before the football homecoming game. Normally, I would have turned down a request like this, but it was a light week of schoolwork and I didn't have much else to do. If nothing else, I figured that the cruise would at least have an open bar. A few seconds after I received the email, I replied and secured my spot on the Old Grad dinner cruise.

I met the other selected cadets at 1700 at Central Guard Room, and then we walked down to the docks. As we passed Mahan Hall and began walking down the hill towards South Dock, I was blown away by what I saw.

The dinner cruise was not aboard a standard 35-foot Hudson cruise liner. Instead, it was aboard a 160-foot super yacht. The yacht was breathtaking and unlike anything I ever saw before. It was straight out of *Lifestyles of the Rich and Famous*. The hull was pristinely painted in black with gold accents. On the back of the yacht, there was a crane attached to two jet skis and on the upper deck was a helicopter—a freaking helicopter!

We waited for the old grads to join us and then boarded the yacht. Once on board, we got a tour from the captain.

The yacht was famous. We learned that it was customed built and designed by the ultra-wealthy Forbes family, as in *Forbes Magazine*. The family used the yacht to entertain business executives, heads of state, and celebrities. Past guests of the yacht were a veritable who's who list of the most famous people of the 1980s—Paul McCartney, Elizabeth Taylor, Margaret Thatcher, Harrison Ford, Henry Kissinger, and many more. On this occasion, it was used to entertain prominent West Point alumni and a few less prominent West Point cadets.

The outside of the yacht was gorgeous. It made me want to recite the Ring Poop: "What a crass mass of brass and glass! What a bold mold of rolled gold! See how it sparkles and shines! It must have cost you a fortune! May I touch it please!?!?"

Inside, the yacht looked more like a museum than a boat. The dining rooms, lounge areas, and bridge had ornate decor, the walls had paintings by famous French impressionists, the decks were pristine hard wood maple, the library had many leather-bound books, and the galley smelled of rich mahogany.

I had never been in a mansion, but I imagined that the yacht was similar to one, only on water. It was the most beautiful boat I had ever seen.

After a short tour of the yacht, we departed West Point to begin a four-hour cruise to New York City.

From the moment we arrived, a team of waiters, butlers, and deck hands eagerly served our every need. At the beginning of the cruise, a server introduced herself to me and asked, "Good evening sir. Could I get you something to drink? Perhaps a soda, beer, wine, or something else?"

"Yes, ma'am," I told her. Cadets were taught to call everyone sir or ma'am and this was probably the first time that the 25-year-old waitress was called ma'am, especially on a yacht that regularly catered towards billionaires and celebrities. "Wine would be nice."

"Excellent. Would you like to see the wine list, or do you know what you would like?"

At the time, I didn't know much about wine other than the names of the more popular wine varieties. "Do you have a Pinot Grigio, ma'am?"

Of course, a multimillion-dollar super yacht had Pinot Grigio!

"Yes, sir. I'll bring you a glass of Pinot Grigio right away."

"Thank you, ma'am." She smiled.

In what seemed like 30 seconds later, I had a glass of wine in my hand. It was the most smooth and delicious wine I ever had. From that evening forward, I could never drink Sutter Home wine again.

For the rest of the night, my glass never got less than half empty. If I took a couple of sips of wine, a server was waiting in the wings to refill it the moment that I was not looking.

In addition to the wine, the eight-course dinner was amazing. Dish after dish, we had delicious hams and cheeses, crisp and colorful wild salad, sausage and handmade pasta, lamb lollipops, creamy risotto, and a desert that put the mess hall to shame.

After dinner, we mingled on the deck with the Super Intendent and Old Grads. We smoked Cuban cigars and drank 18-year-old scotch as the New York City skyline slowly passed by.

The old grads were great. Most of them were civilians and most were executives or CEOs at large companies. They shared their West Point stories from decades before and offered professional advice. Many of the old grads instructed us to reach out to them in the future if we ever needed anything. As a cadet, I could never imagine any reason why I would need to talk to a senior corporate executive. In my naivety, I never followed up on any of those relationships.

My evening aboard the yacht was surreal, and the feeling I had that evening is difficult to explain. A few years ago, a friend of mine shared a story which helped me put my experience into perspective.

My Argentinian friend shared with me a story from her childhood. Before migrating to America, my friend grew up in the Argentinian countryside—the poorest of the poor regions in her home country.

She said that as a poor child, she visited her middle-class family in the city. When her cousin, who was the same age as her, showed my friend her bedroom, she was stunned. The bedroom had toys that my friend had never seen before. She later learned that these toys were called "Barbie Dolls."

As a poor child in the countryside, my friend grew up playing with stick figures made from burlap and twigs. They did not have a television or running water and rarely had electricity. Compared to the burlap and twigs that she played with, the Barbies and other toys looked like alien technology. Up until that moment in her life, my friend never knew that things like Barbie Dolls existed.

In many ways, my experience on the yacht made me feel like my Argentinian friend. After growing up in a humble middle-class family for 20 years, I didn't know that things like the Forbes super yacht existed.

Sure, I watched shows like *Lifestyles of the Rich and Famous* and *MTV Cribs*, but watching one of those shows and actually experiencing it are completely different. On the TV, you can't taste the lamb lollipops or appreciate just how much better Grand Cru French Wine is than Sutter Home.

My experience aboard that yacht introduced me to the physical things that wealth can buy—exotic foods, premium wine, jet skis, personal helicopters, celebrity friends, etc. In addition to the material things, the experience also showed me how wealth can give you unparallel experiences and opportunities.

I had visited New York dozens of times as a cadet but experiencing the New York City skyline from the deck of a super yacht, while drinking Scotch whiskey with Fortune 500 executives and my cadet classmates, was an altogether different experience. It was vaguely similar to my previous experiences on Hudson cruise lines, but at an unparallel level of intensity and emotional richness. Although I was able to attend the cruise for free, I know that most of the alumni were only invited because they attained a high level of professional and financial success.

I strive to save and invest because I know that building my net worth will allow me to live a richer and more rewarding life. The figure in my bank account has an emotional feeling attached to it. It's a feeling of freedom; the freedom to have carefree, intense, and rewarding experiences.

Of course, you can have great experiences without spending any money. Some of my most memorable experiences cost me barely any money. But, at the same time, many of my most memorable experiences cost me a lot of money. Wealth gives you options to choose different types of experiences.

If you want to be a millionaire or a billionaire, you need to have an emotional connection to your financial goals. The stronger that emotional connection, the more likely you will be to achieve your financial goals.

For some people, their goal for wealth is to give their children a better life, to buy a beach house in Hawaii, travel the world after they retire, or start a business after the military. For me, my goal is to live everyday like I'm on a super yacht. I want every day to feel like a blessing, full of rich experiences and surrounded by great people, and I want to pass on similar opportunities to my children.

Whatever your goal, you need to have a strong purpose other than making money for the sake of making money. You need to have a goal for why you want to make money and you need an emotional attachment to that goal.

LET'S RECAP

Your financial goals should have and emotional connection. The stronger the emotional connection, the more likely you will be to achieve your goals.

Wealth gives you freedom. Although wealth is not required to live a rich and rewarding live, wealth gives you more options to live a spectacular life.

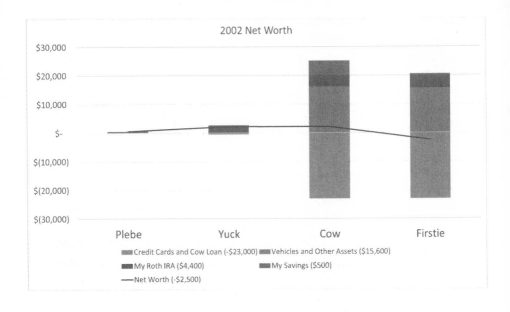

BUDGETS

After graduation, I had to serve a minimum of five years in the Army as part of West Point's service obligation.

I was a mediocre cadet. I had more than a few demerits on my record and I was ranked around 450 in our class, right around the median. I really wanted to branch Army Aviation and fly Apaches but I was afraid that I would get my second choice, Corps of Engineers, instead.

I put Aviation first on my list and on Branch Night, I got lucky. I made the cut off for Aviation.

After graduation, and a full 60 days of leave, I headed to flight school in lower Alabama.

Fort Rucker was hot, humid, and far away from any major metropolitan area. Coming from New York, Alabama was shocking. It was my first-time seeing cars and stores proudly displaying the Confederate flag. Fort Rucker was the kind of place where locals hung out in their pickup trucks in the Walmart parking lot on Friday nights.

I wasn't initially a fan of Fort Rucker, but I loved the Aviation branch and the Army. After living as a restricted cadet for four years, I felt like I was finally beginning my adult life. The pay was also great!

I was making about $40,000 before taxes which was a take home pay of about $3,000 per month. $3,000 went a long way in lower Alabama.

I rented a house with four other classmates, which was $750 per month total, or about $188 per person. I paid $430 each month to repay my Cow Loan, and another $150 per month for groceries. I should have had at least an extra $1,500 per month in disposable income, but I spent it all on bar tabs, weekend trips to Destin, and flying my cadet girlfriend back and forth from New York.

Flight school was challenging. From early in the morning until late at night, we were always in class, preparing for flight line, or studying. We had more freedom than cadets, but the academic workload and stress was similar. I think that is why every weekend we always partied or drove down to the beach in Destin or Panama City. The weekends were a way to relieve the stress after long and challenging weeks.

It wasn't until the end of flight school that I began to get a little more serious about money. Towards the end of flight school, I got selected to transition to the OH-58 Kiowa Warror helicopter—I didn't rank high enough to get Apaches—and I received orders for Fort Hood, TX. The upcoming move to my next duty station prompted me to sit down and make a budget. I began my budget using an Excel spreadsheet.

When I first started budgeting, I just listed each of my monthly expenses. Over time I added more features to my spreadsheet. After a few iterations, I ended up with a spreadsheet that had a column for planned expenses and another for actual expenses. Each tab of the spreadsheet was for a different month, and within each tab, I bucketed expenses by categories like rent, groceries, gas, dining out, partying, weekend trips, and other unplanned expenses. Here is an example of my spread sheet from when I was a lieutenant.

	A	B	C	D	E	F	G	H
1	NOVEMBER FINANCES							
2	1sy Pay Period					2nd Pay Period		
3		Predicted	Actual	Delta b/w USAA			Predicted	Actual
4	**Bills**							
5	Rent	$ 700.00	$ 700.00			Sprint PCS	$ 76.80	
6	USAA Insurance	$ 112.38	$ 112.38			Gold's Gym	$ 32.46	
7						Electric	$ -	
8	Utilities	$ 53.77	$ 53.77					
9	Roth IRA	$ 100.00	$ 100.00			Roth IRA	$ 100.00	
10	Mutual Fund	$ 50.00	$ 50.00			Mutual Fund	$ 50.00	
11		$ 1,016.15	$ 1,016.15				$ 259.26	$ -
12								
13	**Credit Cards**							
14								
15	DELL	$ 75.00	$ 75.00			Cow Loan	$ 395.18	
16	USAA Master Card	$ 50.00	$ 50.00			USAA Master Card		
17	PFCU Master Card					PFCU Master Card	$ 230.00	
18	Bank of America	$ 50.00	$ 50.00			Bank of America		
19	Star Card	$ 10.00	$ 10.00			Star Card		
20		$ 185.00	$ 185.00				$ 625.18	$ -
21								
22	**Predictable Expenses**							
23	Groceries	$ 62.20	$ 62.20			Groceries	$ 100.00	
24	Dining	$ 135.12	$ 135.12	$ (12.53)		Dining Out	$ 75.00	
25	Gas	$ 98.02	$ 98.02			Gas	$ 40.00	
26	Movies					Movies	$ 20.00	
27	ATM					ATM	$ 100.00	
28	Parties	$ 61.00	$ 61.00			Parties & Going Out	$ 50.00	
29	Pet	$ 25.60	$ 25.60			Pets	$ 15.00	
30	Subtotal	$ 381.94	$ 381.94			Subtotal	$ 400.00	$ -
31								
32	**Military Expenses**							
33	Uniforms & Equipment					Uniforms & Equipment		
34	Cup and Flower					Farewell Gift	$ 10.00	
35	Dining In and Outs					Dining In and Outs	$ 25.00	
36	Subtotal	$ -	$ -			Subtotal	$ 35.00	$ -
37								
38	**Less Predictable Expenses**							
39	Montreal Hotel	$ 200.00	$ 200.00			Unexpected Expenses	$ 200.00	
40	Car Maintenance	$ 165.41	$ 165.41					
41	Birthday Gift	$ 105.84	$ 105.84					
42	Winter Clothes	$ 158.18	$ 158.18					
43								
44	Subtotal	$ 629.43	$ 629.43			Subtotal	$ 200.00	$ -
45								
46	**Previous Balance**	$ 645.24	$ 645.24				$ 587.90	$ 587.90
47	Income	$ 2,155.18	$ 2,155.18				$ 2,155.18	$ 2,155.18
48	Expenses	$ 2,212.52	$ 2,212.52				$ 1,519.44	$ -
49	Balance	$ 587.90	$ 587.90				$ 1,223.64	$ 2,743.08

QOL JAN FEB MAR APR MAY JUN JUL AUG SEP OCT **NOV** DEC Totals Net Worth

An Example Budget Spread Sheet

My budgeting technique was not incredibly sophisticated, but it worked well for me. It allowed me to predict my expenses for each month and for the entire year. If I went over my planned budget, I could see how it would affect my budget in the following pay period. My budget gave me the confidence to save for retirement and during the latter part of flight school, I was able to save $1,200 towards my Roth IRA.

There are plenty of different budgeting techniques. Some people use apps like Dave Ramsey's *Total Money Makeover* app, some use complex software like Quicken, others use an envelope system where they withdraw money and then set aside cash in separate envelopes each month ($400 for groceries, $600 for dining, $100 for gas, etc.). My budgeting and spreadsheet system was not particularly sexy. But I made it, I updated it weekly, and I knew my expenses down to the penny. I didn't always keep below my anticipated expenses, but I always knew how much of my income I had spent and how much I would have remaining at the end of each month. It was the system that worked for me.

If you are a junior officer and serious about increasing your net worth, then a budget system is a necessity. If you don't know where your money goes, then you will surely lose it. Understanding how you spend money is the first step to financial freedom.

For the first ten years of my career, I continued to budget using an Excel spreadsheet which eventually helped me max out my Roth IRA each year.

I probably could have saved more during my lieutenant years. Although I maxed out my IRA, I admit that for most of my early career, I slacked on my Thrift Savings Plan. Despite my shortcomings, I know that without a budgeting tool, I wouldn't have saved any money.

In a separate Excel spreadsheet, I also created another document for my lifetime pay.

As military personnel, we are in a unique position because our salaries are public information. Furthermore, we can estimate when we will get promoted and we currently have high promotion rates for the ranks of second lieutenant to first lieutenant and to captain. It is a little more challenging to get promoted to major and lieutenant colonel, but the odds are in your favor that as long as you take the hard jobs, do your best, and don't fuck up along the way, you can get promoted.

Occasionally, the Army will downsize, which can decrease the likelihood of promotion and increase the risk of separation. So, it's always important to do your best at every job and keep an eye on your evaluation reports because you never want to be in a position where the Army could end your career prematurely.

If you plan to make the Army a career, it is easy to predict your annual and monthly salary from the moment you get commissioned through a twenty-year career.

During flight school, I mapped out my salary for twenty years. I estimated my rank for every year of my career. I expected to get married around my seventh year of service. Then, I looked up the base salary, basic housing allowance, and flight pay for each year. All this public info is readily available on the internet. I subtracted my tax deductions and then calculated my annual salary, monthly salary, and major expenses for every year from lieutenant through lieutenant colonel.

As a Cow at West Point, we had a mandatory financial class where we compared options of buying a new, used, or leased car (hint: never ever lease a car). I assume that West Point still teaches that class since it serves an important lesson on the present and future value of money.

My lifetime earning sheet is a similar format to that car comparison exercise. I looked up the pay chart and estimated my rank and pay at each year of my career. I knew that I would live at different duty stations during my career, but was not sure which ones yet, so I used the standard Basic Allowance for Housing (BAH) rates at Fort Hood.

I estimated that military pay would increase at a rate of about 2.5% per year, which gave me a money factor to estimate my future pre-tax income. I then calculated how much I would save each year in my Roth IRA (max allowed) and TSP (10% of my base salary), then applied an 8% annual interest rate to calculate a compounding interest goal for my investments. At 20 years of service, I estimated that I could save over $500,000 in my Roth IRA and TSP.

Factors have changed since I calculated this goal nearly 20 years ago. Over the years, the military has received pay raises between 1.0% to 4.7% per year. Today, a senior LTC makes $9,556 which is pretty close to the $9,462 I estimated 20 years ago using 2.5% annual pay raise rates. When I switched to a Functional Area later in my career, I lost my flight pay. Additionally, I live in the Washington D.C. area now and receive much higher BAH. The housing allowance is somewhat of a wash though since most of that goes to my rent. Still, my estimate was pretty close.

As a second lieutenant, I set a goal to save $500,000 by the time I retired. Today, my Roth IRA and TSP are currently worth $480,000. At the time of writing this, I'm on terminal leave and still have two months before I retire. I estimate that if my investments continue to rise the way they have been, I should hit $500,000 by my official retirement date—it's amazing to have a goal and a plan!

20 YEAR CAREER FINANCIAL PLAN

Year	2002	2003	2004	2005	2006	2007	2008	2009	2010	2011
Year of Service	1	2	3	4	5	6	7	8	9	10
Rank	2LT	2LT	1LT	1LT	CPT	CPT	CPT	CPT	CPT	CPT
Base Pay (Monthly)	$ 2,097	$ 2,097	$ 2,751	$ 3,169	$ 3,698	$ 3,698	$ 3,875	$ 3,875	$ 4,070	$ 4,070
Flight Pay	$ 125	$ 125	$ 156	$ 188	$ 206	$ 206	$ 650	$ 650	$ 650	$ 650
Housing Allowance	$ 663	$ 850	$ 900	$ 900	$ 1,000	$ 1,000	$ 1,000	$ 1,200	$ 1,200	$ 1,200
Annual Pre-Tax Income	$ 34,620	$ 36,864	$ 45,684	$ 51,084	$ 58,848	$ 58,848	$ 66,300	$ 68,700	$ 71,040	$ 71,040
Pay Raise %	0%	2.5%	2.5%	2.5%	2.5%	2.5%	2.5%	2.5%	2.5%	2.5%
Money Factor	1	1.03	1.05	1.08	1.10	1.13	1.16	1.19	1.22	1.25
Future Pre-Tax Income	$ 34,620	$ 37,786	$ 47,997	$ 55,012	$ 64,957	$ 66,581	$ 76,888	$ 81,663	$ 86,555	$ 88,719
Annual Roth IRA	$ 3,000	$ 3,000	$ 4,000	$ 4,000	$ 4,000	$ 4,000	$ 4,000	$ 4,000	$ 4,000	$ 4,500
TSP Rate	10%	10%	10%	10%	10%	10%	10%	10%	10%	10%
Annual TSP Savings	$ 2,666	$ 3,779	$ 4,800	$ 5,501	$ 6,496	$ 6,658	$ 7,689	$ 8,166	$ 8,656	$ 8,872
Investment ROI	8%	8%	8%	8%	8%	8%	8%	8%	8%	8%
Annual Savings	$ 5,666	$ 6,779	$ 8,800	$ 9,501	$ 10,496	$ 10,658	$ 11,689	$ 12,166	$ 12,656	$ 13,372
Previous Year Interest	$ -	$ 453	$ 1,032	$ 1,818	$ 2,724	$ 3,782	$ 4,937	$ 6,267	$ 7,741	$ 9,373
Net Account Value	$ 5,666	$ 12,898	$ 22,730	$ 34,049	$ 47,269	$ 61,709	$ 78,334	$ 96,767	$ 117,164	$ 139,909

Year	2012	2013	2014	2015	2016	2017	2018	2019	2020	2021
Year of Service	11	12	13	14	15	16	17	18	19	20
Rank	CPT	MAJ	MAJ	MAJ	MAJ	MAJ	MAJ	LTC	LTC	LTC
Base Pay (Monthly)	$ 4,231	$ 4,696	$ 4,930	$ 4,930	$ 5,092	$ 5,092	$ 5,255	$ 5,755	$ 5,919	$ 5,919
Flight Pay	$ 650	$ 650	$ 650	$ 650	$ 840	$ 840	$ 840	$ 840	$ 840	$ 840
Housing Allowance	$ 1,200	$ 1,500	$ 1,500	$ 1,500	$ 1,500	$ 1,500	$ 1,500	$ 1,800	$ 1,800	$ 1,800
Annual Pre-Tax Income	$ 72,972	$ 82,152	$ 84,960	$ 84,960	$ 89,184	$ 89,184	$ 91,140	$ 100,740	$ 102,708	$ 102,708
Pay Raise %	2.5%	2.5%	2.5%	2.5%	2.5%	2.5%	2.5%	2.5%	2.5%	2.5%
Money Factor	1.28	1.31	1.34	1.38	1.41	1.45	1.48	1.52	1.56	1.60
Future Pre-Tax Income	$ 93,410	$ 107,791	$ 114,262	$ 117,118	$ 126,015	$ 129,165	$ 135,298	$ 153,288	$ 160,189	$ 164,194
Annual Roth IRA	$ 4,500	$ 4,500	$ 4,500	$ 4,500	$ 4,500	$ 4,500	$ 5,000	$ 5,000	$ 5,000	$ 5,000
TSP Rate	10%	10%	10%	10%	10%	10%	10%	10%	10%	10%
Annual TSP Savings	$ 9,341	$ 10,779	$ 11,426	$ 11,712	$ 12,601	$ 12,917	$ 13,530	$ 15,329	$ 16,019	$ 16,419
Investment ROI	8%	8%	8%	8%	8%	8%	8%	8%	8%	8%
Annual Savings	$ 13,841	$ 15,279	$ 15,926	$ 16,212	$ 17,101	$ 17,417	$ 18,530	$ 20,329	$ 21,019	$ 21,419
Previous Year Interest	$ 11,193	$ 13,195	$ 15,473	$ 17,985	$ 20,721	$ 23,747	$ 27,040	$ 30,686	$ 34,767	$ 39,230
Net Account Value	$ 164,943	$ 193,417	$ 224,817	$ 259,014	$ 296,837	$ 338,000	$ 383,570	$ 434,584	$ 490,370	$ 551,019

Half million dollars was the goal I set as a second lieutenant. Today, with the TSP matching and the strategies I outline in this book, I estimate that a new officer entering the Army in 2021 could save nearly $1,000,000 by the time they reach 20 years of service.

I'm sure that there are more accurate ways to calculate the present and future values of money, but for my planning purposes, my simple spreadsheet worked great. More importantly, the calculations made sense to me. Creating a budget and future financial projection is an important step in building a deep and meaningful relationship with wealth. The chart at the end of this chapter provides some current pay scale numbers for you to complete your own estimates.

LET'S RECAP

Budgeting helps you to understand and plan where your money goes. If you want to be a millionaire, you need a plan. A budget is that plan.

A monthly budget should include planned and actual expenses. Throughout the month, you should review the variance between your plan and actuals.

A long-term budget can help you identify financial goals for 12 months, 5 years, 20 years, or more. Since pay scales are public, it's easy for military members to develop long term financial goals.

Estimated Income using 2021 Pay Scale

Years in Service	Rank	Monthly Base Pay	Housing Allowance*	Annual Income
1	2LT	$ 3,386.00	$ 1,149.00	$ 54,420.00
2	2LT	$ 3,386.00	$ 1,149.00	$ 54,420.00
3	1LT	$ 4,443.00	$ 1,290.00	$ 68,796.00
4	1LT	$ 5,117.00	$ 1,290.00	$ 76,884.00
5	CPT	$ 6,023.00	$ 1,530.00	$ 90,636.00
6	CPT	$ 6,023.00	$ 1,530.00	$ 90,636.00
7	CPT	$ 6,311.00	$ 1,530.00	$ 94,092.00
8	CPT	$ 6,311.00	$ 1,686.00	$ 95,964.00
9	CPT	$ 6,628.00	$ 1,686.00	$ 99,768.00
10	CPT	$ 6,628.00	$ 1,686.00	$ 99,768.00
11	MAJ	$ 7,684.00	$ 1,794.00	$ 113,736.00
12	MAJ	$ 7,684.00	$ 1,794.00	$ 113,736.00
13	MAJ	$ 8,067.00	$ 1,794.00	$ 118,332.00
14	MAJ	$ 8,067.00	$ 1,794.00	$ 118,332.00
15	MAJ	$ 8,333.00	$ 1,794.00	$ 121,524.00
16	MAJ	$ 8,333.00	$ 1,794.00	$ 121,524.00
17	LTC	$ 9,293.00	$ 1,890.00	$ 134,196.00
18	LTC	$ 9,293.00	$ 1,890.00	$ 134,196.00
19	LTC	$ 9,556.00	$ 1,890.00	$ 137,352.00
20	LTC	$ 9,556.00	$ 1,890.00	$ 137,352.00

*BAH Rates for Fort Bragg, NC. Assumes BAH with dependents after 7 years of service.

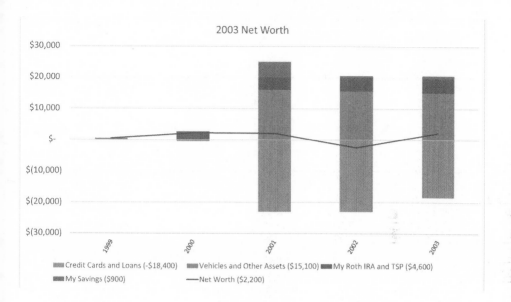

2003 - 2004

FAMILY

I was a first lieutenant and recently graduated flight school, when my cousin called me to ask for money, "Hey Cuz. Work at the restaurant has been slow. It's been a little tight this month. You think I could borrow some money?"

My cousin and I were close. He was like an older brother to me. I had let my younger sister borrow money before, but never expected my older cousin to ask for a loan. "How much do you need?"

"Well, you know, I have to pay rent and Lisa hasn't been working since she had the miscarriage. I was supposed to have a catering gig last week, but they cancelled on me at the last minute. So... uh... you think I could maybe borrow twenty-five hundred?"

Geez, I thought, *I was expecting about $500.*

My cousin continued, "I'll pay you back though. It's going to be wedding season soon and I already have a few jobs lined up. I got a big wedding in two weeks, three hundred people, so that's like $750 dollars right there."

My cousin was 13 years older than me. He was 35 years old, and it shocked me that he would ask me, his 22-year-old younger cousin for a loan.

It seemed like his entire adult life he made bad decisions. He was enlisted in the Navy in his early 20s but got out of the Navy to chase a girl. A few years after leaving the Navy, he started going to culinary school but dropped out for some reason. Over the years he had different catering jobs or chef jobs at restaurants, but he never seemed to be able to hold one longer than a year or two. Whenever he managed to get into the back of the house at a nice restaurant, he always seemed to get into a stupid argument with the manager, or screw up somehow, and get fired.

At one point a few years earlier, my cousin was even part of one of those get-rich-quick pyramid schemes. After repeatedly trying to sell me a bunch of crap

I didn't need and then trying to get me to join as one of his subordinate sales partners. He eventually gave up on it.

As a side note, I knew a few lieutenants who joined these multi-level marketing programs. They are always a waste of your time and money. They are designed to exploit your relationships with friends and family, and you should avoid them at all costs.

Like his pyramid scheme program, my cousin's entire life was one bad decision after another. I'm sure he would pay me back eventually, like maybe in ten years, but I felt like lending him money would just empower his bad decisions.

"Um, that's a lot," I replied reluctantly, "I could maybe let you borrow $500."

"Ok. Yeah, that would be great." He sounded disappointed.

"Give me a few days to get the money together," I said as I mentally reviewed my bank account. I would need to look over my budget to confirm if I could give more.

"Thanks cuz. I really appreciate it."

"No problem," I reluctantly replied.

In the early 2000s, PayPal and cash apps were still not popular and mailing checks was the main way that people sent money to each other.

Two days later, I called up my cousin. I notified him, "Hey, $500 is all that I could afford. I put the check in the mail yesterday."

"Thanks cuz," he replied.

"I'm sorry that I couldn't help you out more." I felt bad that I didn't give him more even though I probably could have.

"It's ok cuz, I figured it out."

Well damn, I thought, *it would have been nice if you figured it out before I sent you $500.*

He paid me back three months later when I visited home.

That was the last time I ever let a family member borrow money.

I have a big family, eight brothers and sisters and dozens of cousins. Most do not have college degrees. Many still live in the hood.

When I was a cadet at West Point, and for a few years after, I occasionally let my younger brothers and sisters borrow money, usually $200 here or $400 there. Sometimes they paid me back and sometimes they didn't. The most I ever let my sister borrow was $700. She paid half back, and then, since I knew she was a struggling single mother, I forgave the other half.

Mixing finances and family can be an exceedingly difficult situation, especially if you earn much more than your other family members. If you begin lending money as a cadet or lieutenant, I can assure you that your family will continue to ask to borrow money until you eventually say no.

I don't remember when or where I heard it, but a rule that I adopted later in life is:

Never lend money to family or friends.

It is harsh, but the sad truth is that lending money to family prevents them from making the necessary life changes or finding the right opportunities to solve their financial problems themselves. Family will almost always ask you for money because it is easy. It is easier than creating a budget, taking out a loan from the bank, or finding a better paying job. The easy solution prevents them from developing the required financial life skills.

Another reason why you should never let family borrow money is because if they fail to pay you back, your frustration as the lender and their guilt as the borrower, or lack thereof, can ruin your relationship. The same applies to going into business with family. A disagreement about money can destroy relationships.

I've seen this happen many times and even know a guy that had to sue his father in court over property ownership disputes. For me, family relationships are more important than money, so I don't ever lend family money or go into business with them—never ever.

Sometimes though, your family may really need financial help and since you probably have a caring heart, you will hate the idea of watching them suffer. No one wants to see their sister and nieces evicted because they were short on their rent. For these situations, instead of letting my family or friends borrow money, I give it to them as a gift. No strings attached.

If you give money as a gift, instead of lending it, you will be more conservative in how much you give and who you give to. Also, if you refuse to lend your family and friends money and instead offer to give it to them as a gift, they will usually be less likely to accept it.

Some family members may try to take advantage of your gift giving, but I've found that most are too prideful to accept handouts unless they absolutely need it. Best of all, a gift of money is less likely to damage a relationship than a loan.

If you find that your friends or family abuse this practice, then be comfortable politely refusing. Instead of giving them money, you could offer them financial advice. You could even gift them a copy of this book!

You would be surprised how many people will ask you to borrow money but will refuse your offers to help them create a budget. Eventually, your family and friends need to learn how to manage their own finances and regularly lending them money will not help them.

Later in life, when my parents began to get older, I began supporting them financially. They unfortunately did not save up enough for retirement and raising a big family left them financially challenged. My parents had small pensions and social security, but that was not enough to support their living and health expenses.

The sad reality is that African Americans frequently need to provide financial support for their parents. Some people call this the Black Tax. There are certainly many White, Asian, and other families that have the same challenges, however, Blacks and Latinos have historically been at a greater disadvantage in this regard. I had some Black classmates that were even financially supporting their parents as cadets. It's unfortunate, but this is another financial burden that many officers from lower income families must overcome.

For years, I tried to get my parents to move out of the Capital Region. I explained to them that their fixed income could go a lot further if they sold their house and moved to someplace like Tennessee or Georgia, but they refused. Despite most of their children having moved away, and many of their friends having passed away, they were adamant about staying in the Capital Region. So, I began giving them a monthly stipend of a few hundred dollars to help cover healthcare costs and I occasionally help them out by buying them a new refrigerator or washer machine.

At the end of the day, it is sad to see the people you love suffer. Sometimes, as with the case of older parents, it is necessary to help them, but when it comes to able bodied siblings, cousins, or friends, I find it is best to let them figure life out for themselves. If you must help them, give them financial advice or a small monetary gift, but avoid giving out loans unless you can afford to lose that relationship.

LET'S RECAP

Lending money to friends and family can ruin your relationships if they fail to pay you back.

If you need to help someone you love, consider giving them money as a no-strings-attached gift. Be prudent in who you give to and don't let your friends or family take advantage of your generosity.

When people ask you for money, offer to help them with their budget, financial management, or job resume. Teaching someone financial management skills and investment strategies are more valuable than lending them money.

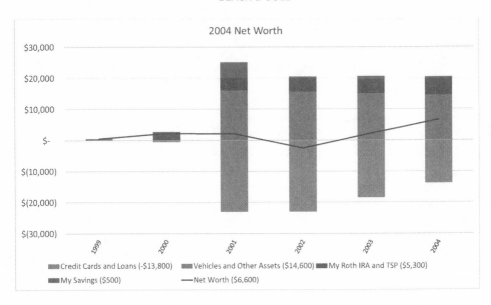

THRIFT SAVINGS PLAN

When I graduated flight school, the world was at war. The World Trade Center attacks happened while I was a cadet at West Point. By the time I graduated flight school, most lieutenants were in combat or preparing for combat.

After flight school, I left Fort Rucker and moved to my first duty station at Fort Hood. As a new lieutenant reporting to the aviation brigade, I knew that a deployment was coming. I reported to the Air Cavalry just after they returned from a deployment, so I had a full year and a half at Fort Hood to acclimate to the regular operational military before our unit deployed again to Iraq.

My lieutenant time at Fort Hood was great. I loved being a platoon leader and enjoyed getting to know our NCOs and enlisted soldiers. As I've gotten promoted, I've had less and less interaction with our enlisted teammates and my platoon leader time will forever be the period in my life where I was most connected to our enlisted force who are the lifeblood of our military.

While at Fort Hood, I made friends with a great group of other lieutenants, warrant officers, and soldiers. I also had a roommate, another lieutenant in our battalion, that I shared a townhouse with in Killeen, TX. When we weren't flying training missions or in the field, we regularly barbequed with friends, hosted poker nights, or explored everything that nearby Austin had to offer.

One weekend, we took a trip to Austin where I met my future wife. She was a marketing student at the University of Texas. The dating scene at Fort Hood was severely limited, so when I found a good-looking girl, who was in school and not a single mother, I did everything I could to woo her. As my upcoming deployment approached, I spent every free weekend I had with her. When I left for the deployment, we decided to give the long-distance relationship a try.

Prior to the deployment, I packed up all my household goods and moved them into storage. During the deployment, I was earning my base salary, housing allowance, flight pay, and hazardous duty pay—all tax free. In Iraq, I lived rent free in a compartmentalized housing unit (CHU) and ate free meals at the dining facility every day. About once a week, I would treat myself to a chai latte from Green Bean or a Pizza Hut pizza, but that was about it. During my deployment, I did not budget, because I barely had any expenses. Almost all my income for a year went straight to my bank account and stayed there.

When I moved to Fort Hood, I took a break from saving into my IRA, but during the deployment I started back up again. At the time, the Roth IRA limit was $3,000 per year, so as soon as I had $3,000 in my bank account, which was the second month of the deployment, I maxed out my Roth IRA for the previous year and invested in an S&P 500 mutual fund. The next month, I maxed out my Roth IRA again for the current year. That year, the contribution limit increased from $3,000 per year to $4,000.

Investing in a Roth account during a deployment is an epic move. With Roth accounts, you pay taxes on your earnings for the year of the contribution (current or previous year). If you hold those funds until the minimum age, your profit is tax exempt. So, if you invest in a Roth account while you are deployed in a tax-free status, you can earn money tax-free and then deposit it in a Roth, and then never pay taxes on that money—never!

There are limits to how much you can earn and still contribute to a Roth IRA. The limit is based on your Modified Adjusted Gross Income (MAGI) as reported on your taxes. Most officers will not exceed that limit unless they are a colonel or lieutenant colonel with dual income from a spouse. Still, it's something to keep an eye on later in your career. In 2021, the IRA contribution earning limit is $140,000 for singles and $208,000 for married couples who file joint taxes. As a single lieutenant, with a base pay of about $40,000 a year, it would be a long time before I needed to worry about exceeding my earning limit.

While I was deployed, I also finally began contributing to my Thrift Savings Plan. The TSP program is a retirement benefit offered to government employees, similar to a 401(k). While a Traditional and Roth IRA are self-managed, the TSP is administered by the government. For IRAs, you get paid and then you decide when you want to transfer that money to your IRA. You get to choose which financial institution you want to transfer it to (assuming they offer IRAs) and you can manage and trade it per your financial institutions policies. In contrast, the TSP contributions are generally set up as recurring deductions from your pay. You decide what percentage of your salary you want the government to transfer from your salary to your TSP account. The amount is deducted from your salary before you get paid. Inside your TSP, you can select from a short list of government administered mutual funds.

Compared to most 401(k) plans offered by commercial companies, the low fees of the Thrift Savings Plan are excellent. The mutual funds available in the TSP are very similar to most 401(k)s, but the administrative fees of the TSP are much lower. The average administration fee for most 401(k)s is between 0.500% and 2.000% per year. In contrast the fees for the TSP average between 0.045% and 0.070%. These fees are usually rolled into each fund's performance, so most people don't see them, but they are there. While a 1% annual fee may seem small, if you save $100,000, a 1% fee compounded over 20 years would be over $22,000 in additional savings.

Keeping in line with my financial plan, I set up a 10% TSP deduction for my base pay and combat pay. In retrospect, I should have contributed a lot more, but in my head, I thought 10% was a good number so that's what I did. Over a year, it came out to about $4,500 in contributions. At the time, the TSP annual contribution limit was $15,000 per year.

In the 2000s, TSP contributions were relatively simple. There was only one type of tax deferred account, the Traditional TSP. Today, there are two types of accounts officers can choose from, a Roth TSP or Traditional TSP. The difference between them is like the difference between the Roth and Traditional IRAs; pay taxes now or pay taxes later. There are differences between IRA and TSP contributions and withdrawals, but the tax advantages are comparable. For junior officers with a lot of future career potential, I usually recommend the Roth TSP.

Due to recent changing in the military retirement system, the government now also offers junior officers contribution matching up to 5% of their base salary. So, if your base salary is $3,000 per month, the government will match up to $150 (5% of $3,000). If you contribute $500 per month to your Roth TSP, the government will match $150 of that for a total monthly contribution of $650.

This is a tremendous benefit. Contribution matching is essentially free money. Therefore, I recommend that young officers take full advantage of their Roth TSP, up to the percentage that is matched by the government. After exceeding that percentage, I recommend that you max out your Roth IRA next. These are general rules of thumb that are good strategies for most junior officers.

Although the Roth IRA has similar tax advantages to the Roth TSP, I prefer the Roth IRA because it offers more flexibility in investment options. Instead of being limited to less than a dozen TSP mutual funds, most Roth IRA accounts allow contributors to invest in the wide variety of mutual funds and stocks available on the major stock exchanges.

After Roth TSP matching is maxed, and after the Roth IRA is maxed, then the next goal should be to max the remainder of your Roth TSP. Currently the max TSP contribution is $19,500 per year and the max IRA contribution limit is $6,000 per year. I acknowledge that maxing out both of these accounts is very difficult unless you are deployed, married to another high-earning professional, or live an incredibly modest penny-pincher quality of life (which I do not recommend). Still, maxing out these contributions is a good long-term goal to have.

When I set up my financial plan, I planned to contribute 10% of my pay during every year of my career. While 10% is good, I actually recommend a different strategy now to junior officers. The strategy I recommend is: Start by contributing 5% of your pay and then incrementally increase your TSP contributions at every pay raise.

My TSP retirement strategy goes like this:

When you get commissioned as a 2LT begin contributing at least 5% of your pay to the Roth TSP.

During this time, you should also strive to max out your Roth IRA.

When you get promoted to 1LT, increase your TSP contribution to 6%.

When you get a pay raise at 2 years of service, increase it to 7%.

When you get a pay raise at 3 years, increase it to 8%.

When you get a pay raise at 4 years, increase it to 9%.

When you get promoted to CPT, increase it to 10%.

At 6 years, increase it to 11%.

At 8 years, 12%.

At 10 years, 13%.

When you get promoted to MAJ, increase it to 14%.

At 12 years, 15%.

At 14 years, 16%.

At 16 years, 17%.

When you get promoted to LTC, increase it to 18% and at 18 years of service increase it to 19%. At this point, your annual TSP contributions will probably be maxed out or close to it.

If at anytime you are able, you should try to accelerate this schedule.

If you plan to retire from the Army and continue working in the corporate world well into your 60s (high tax bracket), then I recommend that you continue to invest in your Roth IRA. If instead, you plan to retire at 60 years old and primarily live off your pension and savings (low tax bracket), then you may want to consider switching from the Roth to a Traditional TSP around the MAJ or LTC timeframe.

As an added level of savings, I also recommend that after maxing out your Roth IRA you increase your TSP as much as you can during deployments. Furthermore, I encourage junior officers to contribute 50% of any combat, special, or other incentive pay to their TSP.

If you follow this strategy, your TSP contributions will steadily increase from about $2,000 a year as a 2LT to the current max of $19,500 per year as an LTC. If you strategically increase your TSP contributions to coincide with promotions and pay raises, you will also not miss the money. You will still take home more money after each pay raise.

As an example, if a senior 1LT's base salary is $60,000 a year and her TSP contribution is 9% ($5,400), then her take home pay is $54,600. When she gets promoted to CPT and her annual salary increases to $65,000, she will increase her TSP contribution to 10% ($6,500) and her take home pay will be $58,500. In this scenario, she will still take home an extra $3,900 per year, while at the same time increasing her retirement savings by $1,100. By increasing your

TSP contributions coinciding with promotions, you'll never even miss the new money that you earn.

In terms of deployments, there are few other non-retirement related financial benefits to being deployed. For example, many deployed soldiers can take advantage of the Savings Deposit Program (SDP).

The SDP is a special savings account that has a 10% interest rate. Soldiers who are deployed for more than 30 consecutive days can deposit up to $10,000 in an SDP. After a yearlong deployment, that SDP would return a profit of about $1,000. Most bank savings accounts offer less than 1%, and the S&P 500 averages about 8.5%, so the SDP is a great, almost zero-risk investment opportunity.

If a soldier knew that they needed a large sum of money immediately after a deployment, or if they wanted an emergency fund, then the SDP may be a great investment option as compared to a regular savings account. However, for the purpose of creating long term wealth, the Roth IRA or TSP is usually a better option due to the longer-term tax benefits.

Another financial benefit of being deployed is that many credit card companies and loan offices will reduce your interest rate while you are deployed. If you are preparing to deploy, I recommend that you call your credit card companies or lenders and request lower interest rates under the Service Members Civil Relief Act. There is a 50/50 chance that you will be successful in negotiating a lower rate. Despite this benefit, I believe that the best strategy is to use your extra tax-free deployment income to quickly pay of any credit card debt.

During my deployment, I didn't take full advantage of my TSP or use the SDP. Instead, I kept all my extra deployment money in an ordinary savings account that earned almost 0% interest. During that year, with barely any living expenses, I earned about $60,000 tax free. My only real expenses were my retirement contributions and a post deployment trip to Playa del Carmen with my girlfriend. At the end of my deployment, I had saved over $35,000.

In a classic financial blunder that you would expect from a private first class, I returned home from the deployment and spent almost all of my savings within a few months. Immediately after the deployment I bought a Harley Davidson motorcycle. For my girlfriend who patiently waited for me while I was deployed, I bought her a $7,500 engagement ring. We spent a few thousand dollars on the security deposit for a rental house and she moved in with me. My fiancé didn't like my bachelor décor, so we spent a few thousand on new furniture and home goods. Later that year, we spent $20,000 on a wedding. The wedding tapped out my savings, so I had to use my credit cards to pay $2,500 for our wedding bands and $7,000 for our honeymoon in the Bahamas.

My fiancé turned wife was still in college, so I was the sole income earner for the house. The only lasting savings I had from the deployment was the $7,000 I deposited in my IRA and $4,500 I deposited into my TSP. In less than a year, all my deployment money was gone, and I had $10,000 in credit card debt—I was a fucking idiot.

LET'S RECAP

The Thrift Savings Plan is a tremendous benefit for government employees. The available funds are like most 401(k)s but the annual administrative fees are much lower.

Under the new retirement system, the Army matches TSP contributions up to 5% of your base salary. If the Army matches your TSP contribution, you should try to maximize that benefit as soon as possible by contributing at least 5%.

As a rule of thumb, most junior officers should begin their career by contributing to the Roth TSP instead of the Traditional TSP.

A good Thrift Saving Plan strategy is to increase your contribution percentage every time that you get a pay raise.

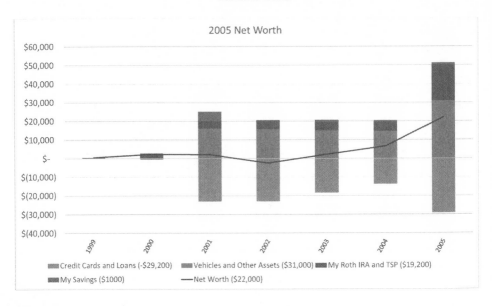

2005 Net Worth

Credit Cards and Loans (-$29,200) | Vehicles and Other Assets ($31,000) | My Roth IRA and TSP ($19,200)
My Savings ($1000) | Net Worth ($22,000)

CREDIT

I've had debt my entire adult life. I can't think of a single moment when I didn't have a Cow Loan, motorcycle loan, car note, mortgage, or credit card balance.

As a plebe, I got my first credit card at an Army football game. During one of the games, Bank of America set up a tent outside of Michie Stadium. They were giving away free t-shirts. The t-shirts had the word ARMY across the chest with an image of an Apache flying over it.

To get the t-shirt, all I had to do was fill out a credit card sign up form. I wasn't particularly interested in getting a credit card, but I loved the Apache helicopter! As an added benefit, when I filled out the form, I got to pick which credit card design I wanted. I picked the one that had a photo of an Apache on it. They suckered me in!

Twenty years later, I still have a Bank of America credit card account.

When it comes to debt, there are many schools of thought. Some people believe that you should avoid all forms of debt, to include mortgages and car loans. Others believe that debt is ok if it can help you invest in assets that have higher rates of return than the debt's interest rate. Others believe in using credit cards only to get reward points. And still others believe that you should take on debt to build up your credit score.

The good news is that if you graduate from West Point, take out a Cow Loan, and pay all your bills on time, you will probably have good credit regardless of your credit card usage. To understand the factors that go into a credit score, anyone can look up their credit report for free at www.annualcreditreport.com. This is important and I encourage you to look up your free report annually.

The free report does not include a credit score, but it does include important information such as credit balances and late payment history. If you pay for a service through a company like Experian, you can see your credit score and get a report on which factors may be helping or hurting your score. Generally though, the free credit report is sufficient to make sure your balance-to-credit available ratio is not too high and that you don't have any late payment history.

Throughout my life, I admit that I am not the best role model. I usually use my credit cards and tell myself, "I'll pay it off at the end of the month," or "I'll take advantage of this 0% APR promotion and then pay off the balance before the interest rate goes up in 12 months," or "It's ok to have a credit card balance at 7% APR because I can invest that money and get a 10% ROI or greater."

There are probably truths in all of these strategies, but at the end of the day, I know that they are lies that I tell myself. A lot of times, I don't end up paying off my cards or my investment gambles don't return the ROI that I expect. Other times, I use my credit card to get points and end up spending a lot more money than I would have otherwise.

Today, my wife and I primarily use an American Express Platinum card for our day-to-day expenses which we pay off in full each month. For my personal expenses, I occasionally run up $5,000 to $10,000 in debt, and then go on a debt free cleanse until I pay it off.

Financial gurus like Dave Ramsey advocate for getting out of all forms of debt, to include credit cards, car loans, and mortgages, as soon as you can.

To get out of debt, the strategy that Dave tells people to use is the *snowball method*. The strategy starts with making a budget, like the methods I discussed earlier, and then requires that you stop taking on additional debt. Basically, you need to cut up your credit cards. Then, you select your lowest balance debt account, for example your credit card, and calculate the max amount that you can pay per month to that card, which must be more than the minimum payment.

You continue to pay your lowest balance debt until it is paid off. After it is paid off, you use that same amount and add it to your next highest balance debt, for example your car loan. After your car loan is paid off, you take the amount you were paying towards your car loan, which included the amount you were paying towards your credit card, and you use that amount to pay off your next highest debt balance, for example your Cow Loan. After your Cow Loan is paid off, you use those amounts to pay off your mortgage or any other debt you have until you have a debt free life. The amount of your budget used to pay off debt never decreases, it only snowballs to pay off the next debt balance until all your debts are paid.

The snowball strategy works because it forces you to create a budget and then the process of paying off consecutively larger and larger debt accounts provides achievable and rewarding milestones. With so many citizens swimming in debt, Dave Ramsey's technique has a tremendous amount of credibility.

While Ramsey's snowball method is uniquely tailored to trick the human psyche, it is not mathematically the most efficient way to pay off debt.

The most mathematically efficient way to pay off debt is to begin with the highest interest rate first. For example, if you had a car loan of $5,000 at 7% interest rate and a credit card with $8,000 at 13% interest rate, then you should make the minimum payment on your car loan and maximize your credit card payment. For most junior officers, paying off the Cow Loan, which is usually about 1% interest, should be the absolute last debt that they worry about paying off.

The Cow Loan interest rate is so low, that I advocate for most junior officers to just pay the monthly minimum until it's paid off. There is not a lot of financial advantage to paying off a 1% debt early since the money would better be used to invest in an IRA or TSP. Credit cards, on the other hand, usually have interest rates between 7% and 20%. For most consumers, credit cards are their highest interest rate debt, so paying them off as soon as possible is a very smart financial decision.

Like the snowball method, you can also snowball payments using the highest-interest-rate-first method. The only difference is that the order of payments goes from highest interest rate to lowest interest rate, instead of lowest balance to highest balance.

For both methods, you can also restructure your debt to get lower interest rates, but you need to account for any hidden fees. For example, many credit cards will allow you to transfer a balance from one credit card to another for a promotional APR of 0%. What these offers do not highlight is that you get charged a fee for that balance transfer and that after the promotional period expires, the interest rate may increase to more than your original credit card. I saw one 0% APR promotion whose interest rate increased to 29.95% after 12 months!

Transferring balances and refinancing loans is a tricky game that requires many calculated decisions. I've known many people who consistently play the game of refinancing loans in failed attempts to get out of debt. Unless you make a budget and live below your means (income greater than expenses), you will never get out of debt.

Debt is a dangerous game, but there are some amazing benefits. One of the more popular cards with benefits is the American Express Platinum card. The

Platinum card includes great perks like 100,000 reward points if you spend $5,000 in the first 3 months, 10x reward points on eligible supermarket and gas station purchases, 5x reward points on eligible travel purchases, $200 in annual airline fees, $200 in annual Uber credit, and—my favorite part—access to Centurion and Delta airport lounges—airport lounges make travelling much more enjoyable!

Credit card companies advertise reward points because 50,000 points sounds like a huge amount. In actuality, one point is usually worth somewhere between half a cent to one cent. So 50,000 reward points is about $250 to $500.

Although the value of a point is miniscule, they do add up. My wife and I usually do all our Christmas shopping using the reward points that we accumulate throughout the year. AMEX also consistently offers great deals to different restaurants and retail stores, like "spend $50 get $15 at Olive Garden" or "$100 to spend at Saks Fifth Avenue." These deals and terms change regularly.

Normally, the annual fee for the AMEX Platinum is $550 per year, but this fee is waived for active-duty military. To get the fee waived, all you need to do is call up AMEX after you get your card and explain to them that you are in the military and email them a copy of your ID.

There are other similar credit card programs. The Chase Sapphire is the most comparable, but the AMEX Platinum is my favorite. As I said before though, credit cards are dangerous, and the AMEX is one of the most dangerous.

The APR on the AMEX can be as high as 25%, which is much higher than a normal USAA or Bank of America Visa or Mastercard. Average consumer credit cards are usually between 7% and 15%. For this reason, I always pay my American Express balance IN FULL each month. Furthermore, my payment is set on auto-pay, so the credit card gets paid off even if I forget about the due date.

Compounding interest works for both investments and debt. If you don't pay off your credit card balance each month, the AMEX 25% APR could quickly bankrupt you.

I didn't have an AMEX until I was a Major. I'm glad that I didn't because as a junior lieutenant and captain, I was not financially responsible enough to own a high interest credit card. My wife and I bought a Bahamas honeymoon with our 7% APR credit card and we were in debt a long time before we paid that off. I'm glad that I did not have an AMEX at the time, otherwise I would have screwed myself.

Credit cards and debt are dangerous, but if you use them responsibly there are some benefits.

LET'S RECAP

Credit cards are financially dangerous. Promotional APRs, point rewards, and incentives can trick you into spending more than you would otherwise.

You should check your credit report annually at annualcreditreport.com. It is a free service and includes most of the information that credit agencies use to develop your credit score.

An officer that pays their bills on time and does not have a high level of debt, will generally have a good credit score.

Avoid high interest rate credit cards unless you are disciplined enough to pay it off each month. If you can pay off your credit card each month, some have great perks. Many of the premium credit cards will also waive their annual fee for military service members.

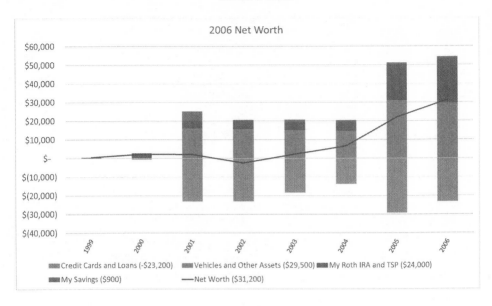

2006 Net Worth

2006 - 2007

RISK

After a short reset at Fort Hood, my new bride and I headed back to Fort Rucker for the Captain's Career Course. The second time around, Fort Rucker wasn't too bad. It was a great break from the deployment cycle and an amazing opportunity to connect with old and new friends.

Hanging out with a large group of my classmates and peers is something that I took for granted at West Point and flight school. In a regular Army unit, you usually only have a few peers in your battalion. Making new friends and staying connected with the ones you have is very difficult. It's especially challenging in high OPTEMPO units. After the deployment and train up cycle, the Captain's Career Course was a much-needed chance to take a knee.

After the Career Course, I PCSed to Fort Carson in Colorado Springs. Colorado was beautiful. There were plenty of things to do: world-class ski slopes, amazing national parks, and gorgeous hiking trails... or so I heard. A few weeks after arriving at Fort Carson, I said goodbye to my wife and my ass was back in Iraq.

I never did become an Apache pilot. I didn't rank high enough in my class to get the coveted Apache training course. Instead, I got selected to fly OH-58D Kiowa Warriors.

The 58D was a squirrely little two-seater reconnaissance and close air support helicopter. It had a .50-caliber machine gun that packed a punch and a rocket pod that rained 2.75" boom-booms. It was also a single engine aircraft and very under powered for many missions. Managing aircraft power and the weight of fuel vs. the weight of ammunition was always a balancing act, but I loved it and I loved the cavalry mission. What they say is true—"If you ain't cav, you ain't shit!"

During this deployment, we were assigned to a task force operating to the west of Baghdad around the area of Fallujah. Fallujah was an insurgent hot

75

spot. It was along the major population corridor that stretched from Baghdad to Fallujah and continued to Ramadi. Around the population centers, irrigation from the Euphrates River fed the area's palm groves and farms. In an otherwise arid desert country, the Euphrates River Valley was an oasis. The area had plenty of vegetation for enemy cover and concealment.

Highway 1 cut through Fallujah and was Iraq's main supply route. Which made it vitally important to coalition forces. The insurgents knew how important it was and fought like hell to disrupt security force operations in the area. During the war, improvised explosive devices and troops in contact was a daily occurrence. As a 58D pilot, my job was to provide the ground force with air cover to give them freedom of maneuver.

Back home, friends and family would ask me questions like, "Is it safe?"

I usually replied with something like, "There are risk, but we do our best to mitigate those risk."

But what I really wanted to answer is, *Fuck no it ain't safe!*

Our task force lost 13 soldiers that year. We had soldiers get blown up by IEDs, aircraft get shot down, aircraft that flew into the ground during brownouts, and another aircraft that crashed after a mechanical failure. If the enemy wasn't trying to kill you, then the sand and 130-degree environment was. Even on good days, we frequently had helicopters return to base with bullet holes. I had a few tracers come close to my aircraft on occasion.

Iraq was NOT safe. If we wanted to be safe, we would have stayed on base and spent our days at the Green Bean Coffee shop, but we had a mission to do.

Our mission was to support the ground force and help save American lives. To accomplish that mission, we had to take risks. We tried to mitigate those risks as much as possible. For example, we had junior pilots fly with senior pilots, avoided flights in inclement weather, preferred night operations when possible, and conducted a detailed risk assessment before each mission. Even though we tried to reduce risk as much as possible there was always some type of residual risk associated with every mission. In many ways, my experience as a helicopter pilot has shaped the way I approach investing.

People frequently ask me questions like, "Do you think Tesla is a good investment?", "Should I buy Bitcoin?", "Do you recommend I buy a house at my first duty station?", "Which TSP fund should I invest in?"

Investing is like combat operations. First, you need to identify your mission goals. Do you want to maintain capital, receive regular dividends, achieve high growth, or something else? Depending on which of these mission goals is your priority will influence which investments you pursue.

Every investment decision also has an associated risk. Whether buying a house, buying stocks, or buying crypto, there is always uncertainty in how that market will perform. You can make money and accomplish your mission, or you can lose money and fail. Either way, you need to take risk if you want to earn more than 1% interest per year.

As soon as you leave the financial security of a fixed interest rate federally insured savings account, you are entering enemy territory. Home prices can blow up, Fortune 500 companies can collapse, and enemies are lurking behind every big money-making scheme.

Unfortunately, you need to take risk to achieve financial freedom. In the world of finances, savings and checking accounts are the most secure places to keep your money. Sure, you can keep your cash under the mattress, but even there you have risk of losing money due to a house fire, teething puppy, or greedy housecleaner. In a checking or savings account, the Federal Deposit Insurance Corporation (FDIC) insures your money up to $250,000 per owner per bank. In most checking or savings accounts, your cash is safe unless the federal government collapses.

The problem with saving money in these accounts is that their interest rates are less than 0.5%. Usually inflation is about 1-2% per year. So, if you stash away money in savings accounts, lock boxes, or under your mattress, the value of your money actually decreases each year because the general cost of living in America increases faster than the measly 0.5% savings account interest rate.

There is a benefit to having a savings account for a rainy day. Investments usually fluctuate up and down, and if you needed some cash quick, it would be unfortunate to need to sell a promising stock on a bad day when it's down 15%. Having a rainy-day fund allows you to ride out the ups and downs of the market without taking out unnecessary credit card debt.

A common rule of thumb is to have three months of expenses saved in an emergency fund. As a lieutenant and captain, I never had more than a month saved up in an emergency fund. Usually, I had zero saved and relied on credit cards to cover emergency expenses. Not a good strategy in retrospect.

As an officer, with a fixed income and job security, I recommend that you save about one to two month's salary for emergencies. More certainly would not hurt, but I always preferred to take any extra above one month's salary and use it to pay off credit cards, car loans, or invest it in a brokerage or retirement accounts. How much I invested, which accounts I put it in, and which equities within those accounts I invested in all depended on my goals and risk assessments for that given asset and that moment in my life.

Most of this book is all about my continuous and ever evolving risk assessment of the different investment decisions I made in my life. As a cadet and junior officer, my risk assessment was simple and naïve (e.g., buying LMT stock because I liked Apache helicopters), but as I've grown and matured, so have my risk assessments.

The important thing to remember is that my investment risk assessments are tailored to my individual goals. I can't tell you with certainty if investing in the TSP, trading GameStop stock, purchasing a home, or buying Bitcoin is a good investment. I can only tell you some of the risks that I see and then I can share my decision based upon my unique circumstances. My salary, cost of living, disposable income, risk tolerance, and expectations for the future will be different than yours. These are all factors that you need to consider when conducting your own risk assessment. Investing is a continuous risk assessment process.

Another important aspect of risk to understand is that risks and potential rewards are usually correlated. The riskier an investment is, the more potential reward it has. For example, an S&P 500 mutual fund is relatively low risk, but the maximum average annual rate of return you'll get is probably less than 15%. Buying stock in an upcoming tech company is higher risk, but the rate of return may be as much as 30% to 50%. At the far end of the spectrum, investing in deep out-the-money call options or throwing your life savings into Dogecoin are extremely risky investments, you could lose everything quickly, but the reward potential is as high as 1,000% or more.

Every investment has uncertainty and risk. I try to keep a diversified portfolio with a mix of high, medium, and low risk-reward assets. I have a lower risk Thrift Savings Plan, medium risk Roth IRA, medium risk rental properties, higher risk brokerage account for day trading, very high-risk cryptocurrency accounts, and extremely high-risk startup investments. I hope that my higher-risk investments will 100x, but if they reduce to zero instead, I'm diversified with lower risk investments.

I've known a lot of people who are afraid to take risks. Instead, they keep all their investments in a savings account and TSP mutual funds. While investing in low-risk strategies is certainly better than not investing at all, the truth is that investing in 100% low risk strategies is a slow path to financial freedom. I prefer to take a little more risk in some areas of my financial life for the chance of accelerating my growth.

I'll talk more about stocks and trading later, but on the topic of risk and retirement accounts, let's talk about the Thrift Savings Plan.

In the TSP, you can invest in a handful of different funds: the S, C, I, F, G, or various lifecycle L Funds. Here is a breakdown of each. The definitions below are copied from the TSP website at TSP.gov.

> The S Fund's investment objective is to match the performance of the Dow Jones U.S. Completion Total Stock Market Index, a broad market index made up of stocks of small-to-medium U.S. companies not included in the S&P 500 Index.
>
> The C Fund's investment objective is to match the performance of the Standard and Poor's 500 (S&P 500) Index, a broad market index made up of stocks of 500 large to medium-sized U.S. companies.
>
> The I Fund's investment objective is to match the performance of the MSCI EAFE (Europe, Australasia, Far East) Index.
>
> The F Fund's investment objective is to match the performance of the Bloomberg Barclays U.S. Aggregate Bond Index, a broad index representing the U.S. bond market.
>
> The G Fund's investment objective is to produce a rate of return that is higher than inflation while avoiding exposure to credit (default) risk and market price fluctuations.
>
> Each of the ten L Funds is a diversified mix of the five core funds (G, F, C, S, and I). They were designed to let you invest your entire portfolio in a single L Fund and get the best expected return for expected risk that is appropriate for you.

One way to think about the funds is that the S (Dow Jones), C (S&P 500), and I (international) are usually higher risk, and the F (bonds) and G (treasury notes) are lower risk. As with most investments, the higher risk funds have higher potential returns and worse potential for loses. If you look at the following chart, you can see that the S, C, and I Funds significantly outperformed the F and G over the past 20 years, except during major market downturns such as the 2008 recession.

TSP Fund Relative Performance since 2003

The L funds are called lifecycle funds and they have a mixture of each of the other funds. The mixture of the L Fund changes over time to reduce the risk as you get closer to your target retirement year. As an example, a L 2025 Fund (about 5 years in the future from today's date in 2021) is about 50% low risk F and G Funds and 50% higher risk S, C, and I Funds. In contrast, and L 2065 fund (45 years in the future) is 98% higher risk S, C, and I Funds. As the target year approaches, risk shifts towards more conservative funds. The following chart shows a comparison of the different L Fund compositions.

TSP's Lifecycle Funds

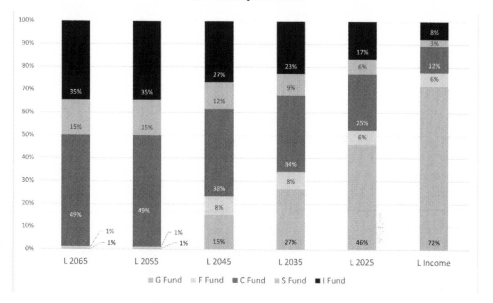

This is how each L Fund is invested as of February 2021

You can invest in your TSP by allocating a certain percentage of your pay towards it through the DoD's payment management website, MyPay (www. mypay.dfas.mil). Once the money is in the TSP, you can select which funds you want to invest in or transfer money between funds using the TSP portal (www. TSP.gov).

If you feel uncomfortable managing risk for yourself, L funds are a great option. A good strategy is to select an L Fund that corresponds to the year you will turn 60 years old. Since I plan on turning 60 in 2050, I would therefore choose the L 2050 Fund. If I want less risk later in life, I could pick the L 2040 Fund, or if I were willing to accept more risk, I could pick a later fund like the L 2055 or L2060. After I retired completely, I would pick the L Income Fund, the lowest risk-reward but most likely to stay consistent through the end of my life.

Alternatively, you could invest in the individual funds if you would rather manage your own risk, or if you had strong convictions about the future performance of the Dow Jones (S Fund), S&P 500 (C Fund), or international markets (I Fund).

I currently invest 100% in the C Fund. Occasionally, if I'm concerned that the market may head downward, I'll temporarily move my funds to the G Fund. Every time I've done this, I've lost money.

Part of the challenge with switching back and forth between funds is that all trades are delayed by about a day. The TSP funds are mutual funds that update their prices once per day. You need to submit a trade request prior to 12:00 EST in order for a trade to execute at the end of day price. If you place a trade later than 12:00, it will be delayed until the end of the following business day.

I've only moved to the G Fund twice over the past twenty years. Both times, it's been when the market was in a steep decline and I was concerned that it would keep going down. My goal each time was to transfer to the G Fund during the decline and then transfer back to the S or C Fund once the market bottomed out. This strategy is frequently called *catching a falling knife*. It is called that becasue it is equally as dangerous.

Both times I've timed the transfer wrong and missed the market bottom. The market began recovering faster than I expected and by the time I transferred back to the S or C Fund, the market was already up higher then when I sold. Both times I've tried to catch the falling knife with my TSP, I've lost 2% to 5% of my account. Most recently, I tried doing this during the Coronavirus pandemic and lost $8,000 because I timed my transfers poorly. For this reason, I usually prefer to keep my funds in the S or C and ride out the ups or downs of the market.

In summary, all investments have risk. Compared to investing in individual stocks, the TSP may be lower risk, but even within the TSP each fund also has different risks and potential rewards. You need to figure out your own goals and the risk that you are willing to accept to accomplish those goals. Once you know your risk tolerance, you can develop a diversified investment strategy that balances risk at a level you are comfortable with. My risk tolerance will be different than yours.

LET'S RECAP

All investments have uncertainty of potential losses or profit. Wise investors should evaluate the risk associated with different investments.

With investments, risk and potential reward are usually correlated. The riskiest investments have the greatest potential reward and the safest investments have the lowest potential reward.

A diversified portfolio should include different asset classes as well as different levels and types of risk-rewards.

Every investor must evaluate investment risks based upon their personal risk tolerance levels and financial goals.

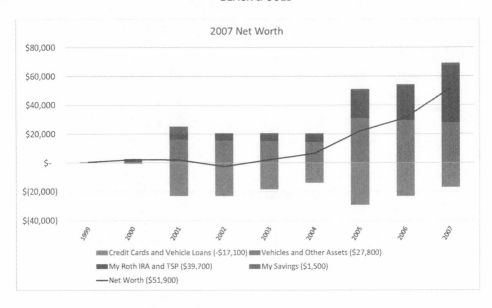

2007 - 2008

BEAR MARKETS

In our flight planning room in Iraq, we always had two televisions playing. One television played the latest bootleg DVD—*Ironman, Superbad*, and *Stepbrothers* were particular favorites that got played on repeat. On the other television, we played the news.

At the end of 2007, I was hanging out in the flight planning room, waiting for a mission, when I remember seeing a breaking news headline that some mortgage and hedge fund companies filed for bankruptcy. I didn't recognize the names of the companies. The news anchor reported some negative trends in the housing market, but since I didn't own a house, I didn't think much of it.

When I got back to my trailer later that day, I checked my IRA and TSP accounts. Each was down about 15% from their highs a few months earlier. When I left Colorado, the economy seemed to growing strong so I expected my account balances to bounce back just fine, and bounce back is just what they did. Over the next few weeks, the market bounced back about 5%.

Then the frequency of news reports about mortgage companies increased as more of them filed for bankruptcy. When I checked my Roth IRA and TSP again, my investments were down almost 30%.

By early 2008, the subprime mortgage crisis flooded the news networks and internet. I didn't understand how the failure of a bunch of greedy investors could affect my GE, LMT, S&P 500, and TSP accounts.

From the time I created my initial Schwab account as a cadet, until my deployment as a captain, I managed to squirrel away about $30,000 in my combined IRA and TSP accounts. Over the years, the investment grew to $45,000 and I was proud of my $15,000 profit.

The sub-prime mortgage crisis hit my accounts and dropped them from a high of about $45,000 to a measly $26,000. After all those years of saving money, I lost $19,000 before I knew what happened. I was sitting at $4,000 less than I had initially invested over the years. I felt like all my efforts to save money for retirement were a waste.

Eventually, the subprime mortgage crisis got relabeled as a recession and President Bush introduced a new financial aid program called a *stimulus*. On top of the national crisis, I had my own personal financial challenges.

My new wife, who I left behind in Colorado Springs, graduated college shortly before we left Fort Hood. After moving to Colorado, no firms would hire her since she didn't have any experience. So, to gain experience, she began volunteering as a marketing assistant at a nonprofit. I was making more tax-free money during the deployment, and didn't have any personal expenses, but I still had to pay for our rent, utilities, car payment, groceries, and other household expenses.

Despite the subprime crisis, I still maxed out my Roth IRA each year and ensured that my wife maxed out hers. When I wasn't deployed, I didn't save anything towards my TSP, but during the deployment I turned that back on again at 10% of my pay. After our IRAs, 10% TSP, and wife's expenses I didn't have much disposable income.

I was a deployed captain making about $70,000 per year tax free. In 2008, I returned home from the deployment without any savings other than what I had in my IRA and TSP. After investing for almost 8 years, I only had $26,000 saved up for retirement, and I was living paycheck to paycheck.

After the 2008 recession, I gave up on my financial goal. I didn't see any way that I could ever hit my goal of saving $500,000 by the time I retired.

I know a lot of friends and family member who also became dejected after 2008. Numerous people took similar losses as me, if not more. For example, my sister had a 529 education plan for her 10-year-old son. As a single mother with an unsupportive baby daddy, she saved over $20,000 for her son's education, but when that balance dropped to $10,000, she panicked and moved the balance from an S&P 500 mutual fund to cash. Traumatized by losing $10,000, she also stopped contributing to her son's 529.

Similarly, a lot of officers and soldiers transferred their TSP balances from the S (Dow Jones), C (S&P 500), and I (international) Funds to the F (bonds) and G (treasury notes) Funds. Some kept their TSP contributions in the F and the G for years after the recession, even after the market recovered. Fortunately, I didn't make that mistake.

By 2013, five years after the recession, the market had fully recovered to its pre-recession levels. Ten years later, around 2018, the market was double its pre-recession levels.

My nephew is now 20 years old. He is attending community college because that is all his mom could afford. When it was time for my nephew to go to college, my sister who once had $20,000 saved for her son's education, only had $10,000 to give him. If instead, she left the 529 in the S&P 500 fund, she would have been able to give her son $40,000.

Ideally, it would have been great if me or my sister could have recognized the impending market down-turn at the start of the recession. If we could have sold high and bought low we would have quadrupled our investments.

Of course, the challenge of selling high and buying low is timing the market. As I personally experienced, it is difficult to recognize a market downturn until it's already too late. Furthermore, once a market is in a decline, it's difficult to catch the falling knife as the market bottoms out.

In retrospect, market corrections like the 2008 Recession occur once every seven to fifteen years. Examples of events that triggered bear market corrections include: the 1990 Gulf War, 2000 Dot Com Bubble, 2001 9/11 terrorist attacks, 2008 Sub-Prime Mortgage Crisis, and 2020 Coronavirus Pandemic. Lesser market corrections occur about every 3.5 years. Since 1900, there have been over 33 bear markets in which the market declined 20% or more.

This is why many people will tell you that you should leave your mutual funds and investments alone and ride out the ups and downs of the market. They say that as long as you continue to contribute to your investments at regular intervals, *dollar cost averaging* will reduce the effects of market volatility on your investment.

As I watched my retirement savings drop drastically and then recover shortly afterwards, the 2008 Recession taught me three invaluable lessons. First, I learned that if in doubt, it is best to continue to invest in stocks or broad market mutual funds throughout market up and down turns. Second, I learned that a steep market downturn is a great opportunity to invest more money, not less. Finally, I learned that selling investments from an emotional place of panic can destroy your wealth.

Market corrections and bear markets are emotionally traumatic events. A few years later, I lost $10,000 in a single day. That was a depressing day and made me feel like a failure once again. These events are invaluable learning experiences and opportunities for self-evaluation. Losing $10,000 in a day prepared me for a future time when I lost $100,000. Instead of panic selling, I learned to keep my cool and make smart investment decisions regardless of my gains or losses. Investing requires a lot of emotional intelligence, especially during bear markets.

LET'S RECAP

On average, bear markets (20% corrections) occur about every 3.5 years. Larger market recessions occur every seven to fifteen years.

It is difficult to recognize a market downturn until you are already well into it. It is even more difficult to judge the bottom of a bear market in real-time.

Dollar cost averaging and continued investment through market up and downturns, can reduce the effect of market volatility on your investment portfolio.

A bear market is a great opportunity to invest more money, not less. Investing throughout a market decline and subsequent market recovery can significantly increase your wealth.

BEAR MARKETS

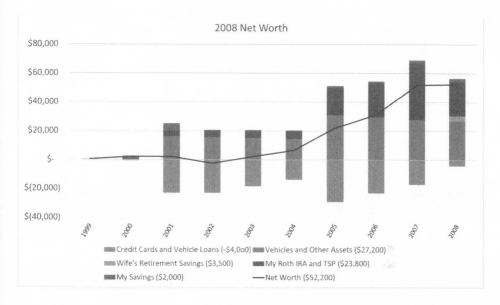

2008 Net Worth

Legend:
- Credit Cards and Vehicle Loans (-$4,0o0)
- Vehicles and Other Assets ($27,200)
- Wife's Retirement Savings ($3,500)
- My Roth IRA and TSP ($23,800)
- My Savings ($2,000)
- Net Worth ($52,200)

BLACK & GOLD

2008 - 2009

PAY YOURSELF FIRST

"I want to get a BMW," my wife said to me shortly after I returned from Iraq.

"Babe," I replied frustrated, "Now that you have a job, we really should be saving most of your paycheck."

I was still driving my dad's ten-year-old pickup truck and she was driving her old Subaru Outback which she had since high school.

She pouted, "It's embarrassing to show up to work in this car."

"Ok. Maybe we can get you a new car, but Beamers are expensive. And maintenance is ridiculous!"

"But we can afford it now," she said with pouty dog eyes.

"How about a Toyota Camry or one of those CVRs. They got really good reviews."

"It's C-R-V," she corrected me, "And no. That's a soccer mom car. I really want a BMW."

"But we really need to save money," I begged, "We could get a used CRV for... like $15,000."

She begged too, "But I really want a BMW and I'm working now. I deserve it."

Over the next few weeks, we had a few more arguments about the car. Eventually, I gave in and we got a new BMW 3 series for about $35,000.

Managing finances as an individual is difficult enough but managing finances as a couple is especially hard.

Mine and my wife's decision to buy a BMW illustrate a common financial trap that many young officers and professionals fall in to. Too many young professionals get their first job or get a big promotion and then they immediately think that they deserve a nice car, house, or vacation. Instead of using their newfound wealth to proportionately increase their savings or investments, they instead use all of their pay raise to buy something nice for

91

themselves. I was guilty of the same trap when I bought a motorcycle after my first deployment and again when we bought a BMW after my second deployment.

This is why it is so important to have a financial plan or to use an investment strategy like the increasing TSP contribution strategy discussed earlier. For any strategy that you develop, you will have the most success if you automate your investment contributions as much as possible. The more automated these savings are, the less likely you will be to spend this money.

If you are a dual-income family, an incredibly powerful strategy is to invest the entirety of your family's second income. In practice though, very few couples do this since it can be very difficult for a dual-professional couple to live off of one income.

My wife and I didn't invest nearly as much as we should have. As a CPT, I was making about $75,000 and as a marketing assistant, she was making about $45,000. We spent almost all our salary each month and then some. As soon as we began earning more money, we immediately increased our quality of life to the max that our income allowed. We still maxed out our IRAs each year, but after the deployment, I stopped contributing to my TSP. She did not contribute to her 401(k) either.

We bought the BMW, and during my reset period after the deployment we took a nice and expensive trip to Aspen. Back in Colorado Springs, we were dining out with friends, going to expensive hipster cocktail bars, or hitting the slopes almost every weekend. About once a month, we also visited Denver for a weekend in the big city. After two back-to-back deployments, we wanted to enjoy our time together—which we did by spending a lot of money. To compound the situation, I had another deployment scheduled about a year after I returned from my second one. We felt like our time together was precious and spent our income accordingly.

During this time, my battalion XO introduced me to a new term: DINKs (Dual-Income No-Kids). My XO was a disgruntled MAJ and whenever we chatted, he always complained about his three children. Usually, he called them "the demon spawn." His boys were 3, 5, and 8 years old. Like many officers, he got married shortly after graduating college and then began having children as a lieutenant.

He constantly complained about how they sucked the life out of him, how expensive they were, and how they destroyed everything. Whenever he had a chance, he told me to wait before having children and to enjoy our time as

DINKs. That's exactly what we did. We were having fun and wanted to wait until after the next deployment before getting pregnant.

To manage our finances, my wife and I created an account for household expenses. We estimated our monthly household expenses, such as our rent, utilities, and dining out. Then each of us contributed a portion of our salaries into a joint account to cover those household expenses. We kept the rest of our salaries in our personal accounts.

At the same time, the country was deep into the recession. My retirement investments were still way down and investing more into our TSP or 401(k) seemed pointless. Our accounts already lost a lot of money and the economy's recovery seemed stagnant. Stocks for companies like Ford, that were once trading at $90, were now trading at $3. My GE stock that I bought at $50 was trading for $10. Luckily, thanks to the war, my Lockheed stock was holding steady at $80. It was less than the high of $100 a few months earlier, but still well above my initial purchase price of $35. There was a huge amount of uncertainty on the direction of the economy.

In terms of making money, the new hotness at Colorado Springs and across the country was in buying foreclosures. After the deployment, it seemed like all our friends were hunting for the best foreclosure deals. We knew people that bought homes that previously cost $300,000 for as low as $225,000. We had other friends that bought cheap $100,000 foreclosures in the bad part of town for $50,000. They fixed them up, and then sold them a few months later for $120,000.

My wife and I didn't buy a house for two reasons. First, we moved from Fort Hood to Fort Carson. In Killeen, TX, the average middle-class home cost about $150,000. In the growing metro of Colorado Springs, the average cost of a home was $250,000. The cost of housing seemed extraordinarily high compared to Texas and we couldn't bring ourselves to take that much risk in an uncertain market.

At the same time, we were also financially strapped due to our lifestyle. We didn't have any savings and had almost $10,000 in credit card debt. Purchasing a foreclosure would have required us to use a traditional mortgage loan that required a 20% down payment. We didn't have that kind of cash.

Today, the average home price in Colorado Springs is $350,000. During the recession, we probably could have bought an average home for $200,000. That's a 75% increase in value in about 10 years. Similarly, the Dow Jones increased from $8,000 to $30,000 during that same time period, a 275% increase. Even if my wife and I invested an extra $20,000 in a Dow Jones index fund during that year, about the difference between a BMW and CRV, today that investment would be worth $75,000.

In retrospect, the recession was a once in a lifetime opportunity to build wealth. My wife and I missed out on a lot of opportunities because we decided that living in the moment was more important than our future. While I do think it's important to enjoy life and relax in between deployments, we probably took the enjoying and relaxing to an extreme and missed out on a lot of good investment opportunities because we didn't have the capital to invest. As we earned more money, we should have tried to keep our quality of life and expenses relatively consistent which would have allowed us to invest more. The strategy of increasing TSP or 401(k) contributions at each pay raise is one way to accomplish this, but neither me nor my wife contributed to our TSP or 401(k) after the deployment.

Despite this, we actually didn't completely miss out on the recovery because we still maxed out our Roth IRAs each year. Although I made concessions when it came to the BMW and our spending, I was adamant that we max our Roth IRAs. In the case of my IRA, I ascribed to the philosophy of *pay yourself first*.

In my head, I imagined my future self at 65 years old. I compared the lifestyle of that future self, to the lifestyle of my parents. My parents barely had any retirement savings. They relied on social security and their small pensions for income, which barely got them through each month. Taking vacations was a struggle for them. On a few occasions, they took out home equity lines of credit to cover unexpected costs like repairing a car after an accident.

I love my parents, but I wanted my future 65-year-old self to be in a better financial position. I decided that in order to accomplish that, at a minimum my future self needed my current self to begin maxing out his Roth IRA each year. So, after the recession, I decided that I would always max out my Roth IRA no matter what. Even if I was living paycheck to paycheck, I would pay my future self first before blowing away the rest of my income. My wife also did the same. That decision was tremendous and is the reason why my Roth IRA is my largest investment account today with the greatest ROI.

My Roth IRA investment grew steadily after the recession. Less than two years after the recession, I recuperated all of my losses, largely due to my Lockheed stock. A few years after that, when I began investing more seriously, my Roth IRA was the main investment account that I used to trade stocks. Today, my total lifetime Roth IRA contributions are about $70,000. I've managed to turn that investment into over $330,000. This was only possible because 13 years ago I made a pact to pay myself first.

LET'S RECAP

Many professionals fall into a common financial trap where they increase their quality of life whenever they increase their income. Instead of falling into this trap, avoid spending all your pay raise. Instead invest a portion of it.

After you set long term financial goals, you should strive to pay your future self first before splurging on immediate luxuries.

Whenever you can, automate your investments using automatic deductions and transfers.

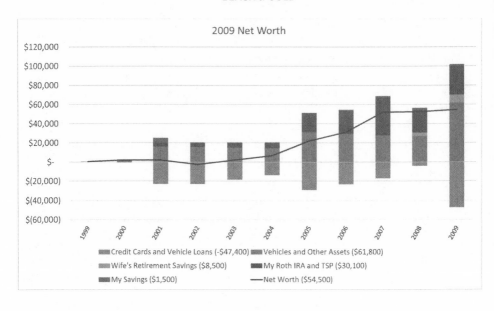

2009 Net Worth

Credit Cards and Vehicle Loans (-$47,400) ▪ Vehicles and Other Assets ($61,800)
Wife's Retirement Savings ($8,500) ▪ My Roth IRA and TSP ($30,100)
My Savings ($1,500) — Net Worth ($54,500)

INVESTMENT LIFECYCLES

"Join the Army and see the world," they said.

They weren't lying—the backcountry of Alabama, arid countryside of West Texas, hot deserts of Iraq, and then the cragged mountains of Afghanistan—real exotic locations!

Combat operations in Afghanistan were much different than operations in Iraq. The environment was different, the threat was different, and my role was different. During my third deployment, I was a senior CPT. Instead of flying missions, I was a current operations officer and responsible for the day-to-day operations of 30 aircraft and over 200 pilots, crew chiefs, and support personnel. I still flew one or two missions a week but managing the task force's current operations was my primary responsibility.

To be successful, in my role, I needed to approach problems from a broader perspective and think about how individual operations fit into the task force's larger strategic goals. While my military position became more strategy focused, I also began to take a more strategic approach to investing. As with my previous deployments, I turned back on my 10% TSP contribution and continued to max out my Roth IRA. Up until that point, I always invested in the TSP L 2050 fund, which coincided with when I would be about 60 years old.

I initially invested in the L 2050 because I didn't really understand the other funds. Without knowing much about the S, C, I, F, or G Funds, the idea of having the TSP program manage risk made more sense than me managing it myself. After the 2008 Recession, when I saw my TSP account nearly cut in half, I decided that I might have better luck managing the risk myself.

From the time I graduated West Point, until 2009, international markets kicked America's ass. In the early 2000s, the newly formed European Union adopted the

Euro which helped stimulate the European market. At the same time, emerging markets were rapidly growing in Brazil, Russia, India, and China, aka "The BRIC."

In the mid-2000s, financial shows like those on CNBC and Jim Cramer's Mad Money, talked about the BRIC similar to how they talk about FANG stocks today (Facebook, Amazon, Netflix, Google).

It's understandable why the BRIC got so much attention prior to 2010. At the time, international markets were on fire and the large developing BRIC nations had tremendous market potential.

When comparing the TSP funds, from 2003 to 2010, the international I Fund outperformed all others. The following graph illustrates the TSP fund performance up to 2010. When I started taking a more active role in my investments, the economy was recovering from the recession and it appeared that international markets had the most potential growth opportunity. So, in 2010, I converted all of my L 2050 balance to the I Fund.

TSP Fund Relative Performance from 2003 to 2010

At the same time, I also rebalanced my IRA. After losing money on GE stock for almost 10 years, I cut my loses. Lockheed was still doing well, so I kept my position there and sold some of my S&P 500 mutual fund in exchange for stock in Apple (AAPL), Walmart (WMT), and a gold exchange traded fund (GLD).

During the recession, the price of gold had doubled. Since the price of gold was relatively stable during the recession, I expected more people to continue to invest in gold as a hedge against future recession risks.

Additionally, I invested in a Spanish telecommunication company called Telefonica (TEF). Telefonica owned most of the market in Latin America, so I thought they would be a great company to capitalize on the growth in countries like Brazil.

In the technology field, there is a concept called the Technology Adoption Lifecycle. The theory says that when adopting a new technology or trend, society behaves in a predictable manner. There are a small percentage of people who begin using the technology before anyone else, these are the innovators. Then there are the early adopters, the people that are ahead of the majority. After the majority adopts the technology, then there are the late adopters. Finally, there are the laggards, the people who show up to the party late because they were ignorant to the technology or because they were reluctant to accept the change.

Innovation Adoption Lifecycle

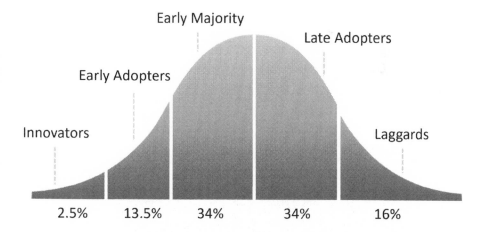

As I've gained more experience in investing, I've learned that investing follows a similar pattern. Whenever a new investment opportunity or trend arises, there are innovators, early adopters, the majority, and laggards. Like the technology adoption lifecycle, the first movers and early adopters usually get the most benefit and greatest ROI from their investments.

As an example, my friend in Colorado Springs, who was the first person I knew to buy a foreclosed house during the recession, got the best deal. He bought his home for almost 50% less than the high a few months earlier. As the foreclosure frenzy continued, the returns on investment gradually returned to normal foreclosure levels with people saving about 10% to 20% on average.

When I bought General Electric stock in the early 2000s, I was a laggard. By the 2000s, General Electric was in decline. There refrigerators and microwaves were no longer innovative and their market growth plateaued. Subsequently, the stock price declined.

In contrast, I stumbled into Lockheed as an early adopter. Although Lockheed is an old company, they were a defense industry pioneer during the Global War on Terrorism. When the Cold War ended and the age of GWOT began, Lockheed was in the perfect place to produce helicopter avionics, C-130 aircraft, F-22 fighters, and drones. I bought LMT stock as an early adopter of this trend. I wish I could say it was because I had the foresight to know that their technology would be vital to national defense, but really it was just because I liked one of their products, the Apache Longbow radar. Then, I rode the wave from $21.80 to $195, a 9x ROI.

In 2010, when I converted all of my TSP to the I Fund, I was chasing the growth in the international markets. From 2003 to 2010, the I Fund was the best performing fund as international markets grew faster than U.S. markets. At the time, the C Fund (following the S&P 500), was the worst performing fund. It performed even worse than the F and the G Funds as it struggled to recover from the recession. However, 2010 was a turning point and for the next decade the S and the C Funds blew past all other. For about half that time, I missed out on those gains because I was still in the I Fund waiting for the international markets to take off again, which they never did.

TSP Fund Relative Performance from 2010 to 2021

The trend of investment lifecycles repeats itself over and over again, with the earliest investors having the greatest profits and the later investors having the least.

As a rule of thumb, I like to think about potential rates of return as a function of how many people doubt an asset. If you invest in a company or trend when few people believe in it and when risk is highest, then your potential rates of return will be greatest.

Table: Estimated Rates of Return for Innovation Adopters

Type of Investor	Risk	Max ROI
Innovator (0 - 2.5%)	Extremely High	100x+
Early Adopter (2.5 - 16%)	Very High	5x to 10x
Early Majority (16% - 50%)	High	2x to 5x
Late Majority (50% - 84%)	Moderate	0 to 2x
Laggards (84% - 100%)	Low	Negative ROI

In the technology adoption lifecycle, the percentage of adopters in each phase are the percentage of the population that adopts the technology. In the investment lifecycle, the percentage is the total number of investors who will invest in an investment over that asset's lifetime.

The reason why laggards will usually lose money is because most investments are a Ponzi Scheme. Early investors make money only if future investors join the party. In the game of investing, you never want to be the one holding an asset when demand for that asset is in decline. Ideally, you want to invest as demand is beginning to increase and sell when demand is at its highest.

The key takeaway here is that if you want to invest and get a 10x or 100x return, you need to identify the next big trend before the rest of the market does. Then take risk and invest in those companies or trends before they become accepted by the majority of investors. And finally, sell your assets before demand begins to decline. The strategy sounds simple, but it is very difficult.

I can tell you that the first time a friend told me that they were buying a foreclosure during a recession, I thought they were crazy. Similarly, when someone tried to convince me to spend hundreds of dollars to buy a digital "bit" coin, I thought it was the worst investment idea ever. Now I realize that my friends who made these investments were innovators and well deserve their $100,000 profit.

While 10x to 100x success stories are romantic to tell, the truth is that it is extremely difficult to predict which investments will be the next Tesla or Bitcoin. To illustrate this, take a look at 2007 and 2008. In terms of technology, 2007 and 2008 was a pivotal moment in our civilization, not because of the recession, but because of the world changing technologies that deployed right before and during the recession. In 2007 and 2008 these companies hit major milestones.

Facebook launched businesses services
Apple sold their first iPhone
Netflix began streaming services
Tesla delivered its first electric car

If you bought stock in these companies your return on investment today would be 7x for Facebook (since their 2012 IPO), 27x for Apple (since 2008), 110x for Netflix (since 2008), or 210x for Tesla (since their 2010 IPO).

In retrospect, investing in these companies seems like a no-brainer, but in truth, most were greatly underappreciated when they first came out. It is really difficult to recognize or fully understand a trend before the rest of the market. It is hard to be an innovator or early adopter.

For example, take the previously mentioned list. I dismissed all of these trends in 2008.

In 2008, Facebook was still a growing social network. People shared photos and life updates on Facebook. Facebook wasn't used for business and I would never have imagined companies paying for advertising on the platform.

In 2008, my T-Mobile Sidekick phone was much better than the new iPhone. My Sidekick had a full QWERTY keyboard. A touch screen phone reminded me of the old worthless Blackberry Palm Pilot that they issued to us as cadets at West Point.

In 2008, I got DVDs from the local Redbox. We didn't have internet on our TVs and I never watched movies on my computer unless I was deployed, in which case I had a treasured external hard drive with a few hundred bootleg movies on it. Internet TV seemed like a useless service.

In 2008, I never even heard of Tesla. I didn't hear about Tesla until 2012. It wasn't until about 2014 that I even saw one on the road.

If I would have been an early investor in these companies, I would already be a multi-millionaire. A mere $10,000 investment in Netflix or Tesla at their IPOs would be worth over one million dollars today.

Of course, it is great to catch a new trend as an innovator or early adopter, but those positions can be extremely risky. For every Facebook, there are 100 failed social media platforms like MySpace or HotOrNot.com. High risk investments have great ROI potential, but they also have a high probability of becoming worthless.

While it's difficult to identify emerging opportunities to be an early investor in, it's equally difficult to know if you are in the early majority, late majority, or laggards. Take for example Tesla. Tesla delivered their first car in 2008; they IPOed in 2010. In 2010, most people still had never heard of the company. Beginning around 2015, Tesla became more popular and that's when early majority investors like myself began to jump aboard Elon Musk's rocket ship.

Here is the interesting part. In 2018 to 2019, it looked like Tesla was past its peak. They struggled tremendously to produce the Model 3, they were burning hundreds of millions of dollars per year, and many investors lost faith. The stock price dropped from an equivalent of $70 per share to $40 per share. It looked like anyone willing to invest in Tesla in 2018 to 2019 was a late majority or laggard, but that couldn't be further from the truth.

In actuality, the people who bought shares of Tesla in 2018 to 2019 were still part of the early majority. Tesla had a lull, but still had a tremendous amount of growth ahead of it. Over the next two years, Tesla rose from $40 per share to over $800 per share, a 20x bagger.

Today, Tesla is riding all-time highs, but there is no way of knowing if the stock price has peaked and will drop to $400 tomorrow, or if it still has another 20x to grow. I'm personally hoping for another 4x over the next decade. Therein lies the biggest challenge of investing—you can never predict with full certainty the future direction of an investment.

At the time of writing this, a very interesting trend is *meme stonks* (an amusing euphemism). Large online communities like the Reddit forum *Wall Street Bets,* have managed to cause rapid market swings through crowd investing. In the examples of GameStop (GME), AMC Movies (AMC), and Naked Brand Group (NAKD), a group of non-institutional investors recognized an opportunity for a *short squeeze.* In other words, they recognized that by rapidly investing in a company en masse, they could drive up the price by taking advantage of hedge fund short positions against the companies.

The real estate market, crypto currency, international markets, and stocks I mentioned are investment trends that take years or decades to go through a full investment life cycle. In contrast, these short squeezes and meme stonks have gone through their investment lifecycle in a week or less. Assuming that these Wall Street Bets investors sold near the highs, the early investors in the GME short squeeze got 100x ROI, the early majority got 10x to 2x, and the late majority and laggards broke even or lost money.

The main man who started the GME short squeeze, he goes by the username *DeepFuckingValue,* turned his $50K investment into $22M. That shows how powerful early adoption can be. That's a 440x ROI!

These meme investment lifecycles happened so rapidly that by the time I learned about them, I was already in the majority. For the most part I sat on the sidelines and watched because I knew that as a late majority investor, the best ROI I could expect was 2x. For me, these extremely volatile and risky trends were not worth the risk, but I am happy for the early investors who were able to make a killing at the expense of over-leveraged hedge funds. I am morally opposed to short sellers and love to see them lose.

Personally, I try to diversify my investments across the investment lifecycle. In my portfolio, I usually invest in a few large companies that are approaching their peak, for example, Amazon (AMZN), Apple (AAPL), Microsoft (MSFT), and Tesla (TSLA). I think these companies are at the point where the majority of investors have accepted them as good investments. My goal for these investments is 2x to 5x in ten years.

Then I have investments in a few companies that are popular, but maybe not as popular as the previously mentioned ones. These are companies like Nvidia (NVDA), Advanced Micron Devices (AMD), and Taiwan Semiconductor Manufacturing (TSM). I still think they have a lot of room to grow, so I consider myself an early majority investor in these companies. Although these companies are mature, they are not front and center on the average investor's radar unless you are into semiconductors, artificial intelligence, crypto-mining, or gaming. My goal for these investments is for at least one company to 5x to 10x in ten years.

Next, my riskier innovative investments include obscure, relatively unknown companies like Lemonade Insurance (LMND), AbCellera biotechnologies (ABCL), and UpStart Holdings (UPST). Most people have never heard of these companies, but I think that they will be very disruptive in their industries. Their revenue has also been growing at a rate of 40% or more year-over-year which I use as a measure of their growth potential. These companies are high risk, and their stock prices also have high valuations, but I hope that at least one will 10x in ten years. Most of my initial investments in these companies is about $5,000 to $10,000 which will hopefully yield me $100,000+ in the next decade.

In my investment portfolio, I also have an even higher risk private company startup investment. I met the founder of the company through my network and invested $5,000 in his nascent company. I am almost certain that the company will fail, but if the founder can pull off a miracle, I dream of a 20x return or more.

Although each of these companies are in different phases of their lifecycle, I like these companies because I think they are part of a broader technology trend—artificial intelligence. It is possible to have trends within trends and artificial intelligence is the real trend that I am betting heavily on as an early adopter.

Cryptocurrency also has its own investment life cycle. In the crypto realm, the entire sector is reaching a point where early adopters are beginning to invest in it. But within crypto, individual coins have their own adoption cycle.

The most mature assets are Bitcoin (BTC) and Ethereum (ETH). Although crypto is a risky market overall, these coins have the lowest risks within the market. My goal with these investments is a 2x to 10x.

Newer, more risky assets include alternative coins like Algorand (ALGO), Stellar Lumens (XLM), Graph (GRT), or Caradano (ADA). These alt coins have the highest risk-reward. I'll occasionally invest in alt coins, but these markets are very volatile, the number of alt coins is overwhelming, my knowledge in alt coins is limited, and the risk exceeds my tolerance, so I usually avoid alt coins. At most, I invest 25% or less of my crypto portfolio in alt coins.

Crypto is too risky for many investors, and that is ok. You can certainly become a millionaire by investing in low-risk investments. As I discussed earlier, a 2x return every ten years can compound at magical rates if you begin investing early in life. And in fact, I encourage people to keep a majority of their net worth in low risk, steady growth investment classes like the S&P 500 or real estate. However, if you want to accelerate your financial growth, you should consider taking occasional risks and try to invest some of your wealth in emerging market trends.

You will need to develop your own investment strategies based upon your personal risk and reward preferences. For me, a diversified risk and lifecycle strategy has been extremely rewarding. My low-risk investments provide stable and steady growth, while my high-risk investments increase in value by occasional leaps and bounds. Many of my high-risk investments barely break even, and many loose me money, but my few occasionally successful high-risk investments more than make up for my losses.

LET'S RECAP

If you want great returns on investments, you need to take risk and invest in market trends and companies before the majority of investors.

Identifying great investment opportunities before anyone else is difficult to do. The investments with the greatest potential returns are generally high risk and may initially seem like bad ideas.

High risk investments can quickly lose money; therefore, you should diversify your investments between different risk and reward levels.

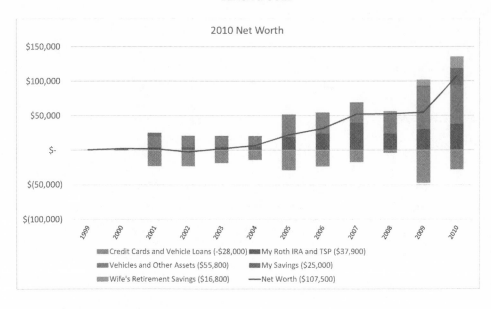

2010 Net Worth

Legend:
- Credit Cards and Vehicle Loans (-$28,000)
- My Roth IRA and TSP ($37,900)
- Vehicles and Other Assets ($55,800)
- My Savings ($25,000)
- Wife's Retirement Savings ($16,800)
- Net Worth ($107,500)

DIVORCE

Halfway through my deployment in Afghanistan, I started to plan my follow-on assignment. I started by calling my Aviation branch human resources officer.

"Hey MAJ Smith, I'm calling from Afghanistan. I'm coming up on my PCS window and I'm just curious what assignments may be available to me next summer."

"Hold on, let me pull up your record."

After ten seconds, MAJ Smith replied, "Let's see. You're already promotable to major and you're an S-3 already. Um, I think I can send you to one of the training centers, NTC or JRTC."

"Anything else?" I begged, "You know, honestly, after spending a year in Afghanistan, NTC or JRTC are going to be hard on the family. I mean, I'll go to one of those if I need to, but if you have something else..."

MAJ Smith replied, "Sorry, but we need OCs at NTC and JRTC."

"Alright, thanks," I replied, *Thanks for nothing.*

The Army has two primary training centers, the National Training Center (NTC) and the Joint Readiness Training Center (JRTC). Army units deploy to these training centers for weeks or months at a time to test their tactics against Army red teams. Although most Army units rotate though the training centers on a temporary basis, each training center has a cadre of red team leaders and Observer Coaches (OCs). This OC position is the one that my human resources officer wanted me to fill.

Although I would have been happy mentoring and coaching junior officers and soldiers, the locations of the assignments are what concerned me.

The National Training Center is located in the hot and arid desert of Fort Irwin, CA. One of the reasons why it is such a popular training center for the military is because the environment is similar to the desert of Iraq.

On the other side of the country, the Joint Readiness Training Center is located in Fort Polk, LA. While Fort Irwin is surrounded by miles and miles of rocks and sand, Fort Polk is surrounded by swamps, alligators, and mosquitos. At both Fort Irwin and Fort Polk, the summers are hot, long, and oppressive.

After multiple deployments to Iraq and Afghanistan, I did not want to go to either location and I knew that my wife would divorce me if I forced her to move from Colorado Springs to Fort Polk or Fort Irwin.

At the same time, the Army launched a new program called the Voluntary Transfer Incentive Program. VTIP allowed officers to transfer from their basic branch to a functional area in exchange for an additional three-year service obligation.

I called up the functional area branch manager, "Hey MAJ Swanson, I'm calling from Afghanistan. I'm coming up on my PCS window and I'm just curious what assignments may be available to me if I VTIP to your branch."

Without skipping a beat, she replied, "We can send you to graduate school. Most of our officers go to the Naval Postgraduate School in Monterey, California, but we can send you to a civilian graduate school if they accept you."

Sign me up!

With a little reluctance, I said goodbye to my beloved Aviation branch and transferred to a functional area. While I was in Afghanistan, I began applying to graduate schools.

Fortunately, I took the GRE earlier in my career during the Captain's Career Course. Since the test results were good for five years, I knew that they would be helpful whether I decided to stay in the Army or get out of the Army and go to grad school afterwards.

I highly encourage young officers to take the GRE, GMAT, or LSAT around the time they are captains. The GRE is for general graduate school, the GMAT is for business schools, and the LSAT is for law schools. Whether you decide to go to grad school through the military or afterwards, it is great to have a test score readily available if an opportunity arises.

I got accepted to a systems engineering master's degree program at Vanderbilt University. A few months later, I departed Afghanistan so that I could pack up my house and family and move from Colorado Springs to Nashville. When I returned to Colorado Springs, I had less to pack up than I expected. After being together for six years, my wife asked for a divorce.

The military lifestyle is hard on families. We usually only stay at a duty station for two or three years before we need to move to a new assignment in a different part of the country. It is challenging to uproot your entire life every few years and start over from the beginning in a new town with new friends and a new job (if a spouse is lucky enough to find a job). In units with high operational tempos, repeated combat deployments with risks of injury or death, adds another layer of hardship.

In the six years that we were together, my wife and I moved three times and were preparing for our fourth. Furthermore, I was deployed for over half the time that we were married. I admit that I may not have been the best husband, but I am certain that the deployments and frequent changes in duty stations contributed to my marriage's failure.

I had a few weeks in Fort Carson to out-process before I moved to Nashville. While I was there, my wife and I saw a marriage counselor a few times, but ultimately agreed that the relationship was unsalvageable. Fortunately, we never did end up getting pregnant, so we didn't need to worry about that, but we did need to worry about money.

When we filed our separation paperwork, we agreed to split our assets 50/50. We also agreed that she would keep the BMW, and stay in our rental house and take over all the household expenses.

During the deployment, we used a joint account for household expenses but otherwise kept separate accounts. Over 12 months, we paid off our credit cards and I was able to save up about $25,000. Earlier in the deployment, we spent $10,000 of that on a two-week R&R vacation to Italy which left me with $15,000.

The day before I moved to Nashville, we sat down and listed the value of our individual assets.

Me		Her	
Motorcycle (pre marriage)	$ 10,000	BMW	$ 28,000
Ford Ranger (pre marriage)	$ 8,000	Roth IRA	$ 24,500
TSP	$ 12,500	Car Loan	(-$ 19,000)
Roth IRA	$ 36,500		
Savings	$ 15,000		
Total	$ 64,000	Total	$ 33,500

We agreed not to add the value of my motorcycle or truck since I had those before we got married. We agreed that she could keep the Beamer and take over the loan. I wanted to add the value of the $7,500 engagement ring to her assets but after doing some research I learned that an engagement ring is usually considered a gift to the wife and not marital property. I disagreed but didn't fight it.

The difference between our assets was $30,500. I also agreed if she decided to move out of the house that she could keep the rental deposit, which was $1800. We agreed that if I gave her $14,000, then our assets would be split 50/50. I wrote her a check for $14,000 and the next day I loaded my truck and drove from Colorado to Nashville.

Managing finances as a couple is hard, and surviving a divorce financially is even harder.

You can argue that I shouldn't have given my ex-wife anything since she had a job and the money I saved was money that I earned from a deployment, but Colorado was a no-fault divorce state. Meaning that regardless of the reason why a couple gets divorced, neither partner is to blame, and each partner gets a 50/50 share of any marital property.

Cutting our relationship and writing her a check for $14,000 was a simple and easy solution that satisfied both of us and avoided debates, agreements, or legal proceedings. $14,000 sounds like a lot, but compared to a contentious divorce, it was a good price to pay for a clean break.

I learned a lot from my divorce. To begin, I learned that one of the best or worse financial decisions you can make is who you pick to spend the rest of your life with. If you are financially prudent, but your wife is a spender, it can hurt your prospects for financial freedom and cause a lot of tension in your relationship. Likewise, if you and your wife are both spenders, you may not have any checks and balances on your spending. This is one of the reasons why I am now a huge advocate for premarital and marital counseling. Even if your marriage is going great, get counseling. Service members can get free counseling sessions through Military One Source.

There are lots of reasons why a couple should see a counselor, but one of the most important reasons is to help make sure that a couple shares financial goals and priorities. Lots of times, it helps to have a third party facilitate financial discussions between partners.

In the end, I don't fault my ex-wife for our divorce. After three back-to-back deployments, I could understand why she was frustrated with our marriage. I just wished that she asked for a divorce before the last deployment.

The year I was in Afghanistan, my income was $100,000 tax free!

I think about how much I could have saved if I wasn't supporting my ex-wife for a year. I could have easily saved $80,000 or more. Instead, I walked away from the deployment and my marriage with a mere $1,000 in my savings account.

When it comes to investments and life, you win some, you lose some.

LET'S RECAP

One of the most important financial decisions you can make is who you decide to spend your life with. You should be sure to marry someone with a compatible wealth mindset and financial goals.

Finances is an important topic that you should discuss with your partner before you get married and throughout your marriage. A marriage counsellor can help facilitate those conversations.

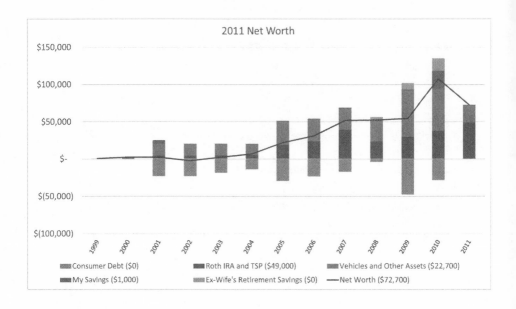

FIRST HOME

After back-to-back deployments for most of my career, two years at grad school was like a two-year paid vacation. Vanderbilt was fucking awesome!

I had a few classes a week, which compared to West Point, were nothing. The math was a little hard, but a few extra hours re-learning the basics on Khan Academy helped me with that. There were a few times each semester around midterms and finals when the workload picked up, but for the most part I had a lot of free time on my hands. I explored the city, went to a bunch of football games, and got back into the dating game.

When I moved to Nashville, I decided to buy a condo in downtown. I really wanted to be in the heart of the city and walking distance to campus. I hired a realtor and told him that I was looking for a modern one or two-bedroom condo that would be a good rental property in the future. We saw about 10 condos and apartments before I found one that I loved.

Everyone has their own house hunting strategy. I've bought three houses over the years, and this is the strategy that I use. Since I usually only stay at a duty station for 2 to 3 years, my goal is to buy a house as soon as I move to a new duty station so that I can begin building equity as soon as possible.

To begin, I backwards plan my timeline based upon my report date. I usually take 30 days of leave in between duty stations, so my goal is to complete the sale and close on my house 30 days before I report for duty. This gives enough time to move to the new city, do any house repairs or painting, move my household goods, explore the new city, and take a short vacation to visit family or friends before reporting for duty.

I plan to go under contract 45 to 60 days prior to my desired closing date, which leaves enough time for appraisals, home inspections, and financing. Assuming that I'm not deployed, I plan to do my first house hunting trip about 90 days before my planned report date. Usually, a house hunting trip is about 3 or 4 days. I hope for one trip but plan a second one about two weeks later just in case my first trip is unsuccessful. For an August report date, these trips would be in May or June.

My research begins about two months before that, or as soon as I receive my request for orders (RFO), which is usually in March. I begin my research by identifying which neighborhoods I would like to live in. This research usually consists of searching the internet and asking friends about the culture of the different neighborhoods.

Early in the house hunting process, I don't concern myself much with the property values, taxes, school districts, crime rates, or any of that. Instead, I rely on general neighborhood descriptions from friends or online forums. I primarily look for neighborhoods where I would want to live in. When I moved to Nashville, I was excited to live in a neighborhood with lots of young professionals in the heart of the city and within walking distance to my school.

Then, I search Zillow to get an understanding of the average value of the type of property that I'm interested in. I run the numbers through a mortgage calculator to make sure I can afford the monthly payments well within my salary. I factor in the cost of annual taxes and homeowner's association cost if I think I will live in a condo or private community. I usually try to keep my total monthly home payments at 25% to 33% of my salary. Then, I apply for a mortgage preapproval. I've always gotten my preapproval through USAA because they are convenient for me but I've never used USAA for my actual mortgage. I always had better experiences working with smaller mortgage brokers.

Next, I hire a realtor about a month before I plan to begin visiting houses. If possible, I prefer to have a realtor referred to me by a friend. Once I have a realtor, I have them begin sending me MLS listings of properties that meet my search criteria. I review these listings everyday leading up to my first visit. I also continue to do my own searches on MLS or Zillow.

Periodically during this process, I email my realtor properties that I like so that they understand my tastes and preferences. A few days before my visit, I send my realtor a list of properties that I want to see. Usually, they are able to schedule visits for about half of them.

It's important to note that I tell my realtor which properties I want to see. The realtor will usually add some additional properties, but I drive the house hunting experience, not the other way around.

Frequently, I hear frustrated house hunters complain that their realtor isn't showing them good properties or finding something that meets their needs. In my opinion, that is not the realtor's job.

I take it as my responsibility to find houses that I want to see. The realtor works for me. I tell them which properties I want to see and then the realtor's job is to do the coordination and scheduling to make that happen. During the process, the realtor should assist with professional advice, price comparisons, and then negotiations.

Thanks to the internet, a house hunter has almost all the same information that a realtor does. You shouldn't' expect a realtor to read your mind and find you the perfect house when you have all the tools to do that yourself. After you identify the properties that you want to see, the realtor schedules property walk throughs and can fill in your schedule with other properties that he or she recommends.

I also believe that the market is self-correcting. If a house is priced at a bargain, it will sell quickly. If it is priced too high, it will be on the market a long time. For this reason, I think that time on market is one of the best measures of how well a house is priced. It is easier to negotiate the price of a house that has been on the market a long time than it is to negotiate a house that is new to the market. Commonly, a really great deal will have multiple offers on the first day it hits the market. It can be difficult to catch these deals, but very rewarding if you do. I bought my third property after finding it the first day it hit the market and that has been one of my most profitable real estate investments.

In buying a house, I also move fast. I rarely spend more than two days house hunting before placing an offer. If you know what you want and have done your research, two days is usually a good enough period to see about 15 houses. If you see 15 houses and none of them appeal to you, you probably have unrealistic expectations about the market or prices.

During the pandemic, housing prices have increased dramatically. Before the pandemic, I bought most of my properties for 5% to 10% less than asking price. Now, it is common to buy houses 10% above asking price. The real estate market is volatile in 2021, but most of my house hunting principals still apply.

In terms of buying a house, it is also important to understand your goals. Most people buy a house for one of these goals: 1) buying a place to call home, 2) investing in a property to building equity, or 3) establishing a rental property to create positive cash flow. A home purchase can share many of these goals, but I recommend that you identify which goal is most important to you before you buy a home. When I decided to buy a property in Nashville, my goal was to build equity, which is the difference between the value of the property and balance owed on the mortgage.

In the early 2000s, I knew two sisters from high school who together bought a tiny apartment in the heart of New York City for $1.2 million. A few years later, that 500 square foot apartment was valued at over $1.6 million. It amazed me that my friends were able to make $400,000 in less than a few years. I hoped that by buying a condo in Nashville that I could similarly increase my equity and net worth. In my assessment, I saw Nashville as a growing city. The real estate near downtown was the most limited and therefore had the most potential growth.

The condo I found was a one bedroom 700 square foot studio in the heart of Nashville. It was less than two years old. It was modern and sleek. It was in the heart of the hip Broadway District and on the 20th floor. It had floor to ceiling windows and panoramic views of downtown. There was an outdoor pool and club room, which in the summertime turned in to a Las Vegas style pool party. Neighbors were friendly and welcoming. The building had southern charm in a chic urban setting. I loved it.

When I saw the building, it was only 75% occupied. Over 90 units were up for sale. The housing market was still recovering from the recession and people were still slow to buy homes. I loved the condo, but I was concerned that the 25% vacancy would make it extremely difficult to rent out when I moved two years later.

I was also concerned by the price. It cost $230,000, which seemed awfully expensive for a 700 square foot one-bedroom studio. In Colorado Springs, that could have gotten me a comfortable three-bedroom house. At Fort Rucker, it could have bought a mansion.

Ultimately, I realized that the price was comparable to the other condos in the area. One of the lessons I learned in moving from Fort Rucker to Fort Carson was that when you move, you need to reset your baseline for how much you think properties should cost. The cost of a house is different whether you live in lower Alabama, Colorado Springs, or Nashville. It can be difficult for the human brain to compartmentalize housing prices based upon location.

I bought the condo using a Federal Housing Administration (FHA) loan. At the time, it was my only option. Traditional mortgages required a down payment of about 10-20% of the loan. After the divorce, I barely managed to save up $6,000. Once I received my dislocation allowance, which is payment that soldiers receive to cover the cost of changing duty stations, I barely had enough money to cover the 3.5% down payment required by the FHA.

A loan from the Department of Veteran's Affairs (VA) was another option, but for buying apartments and condos, the VA loan requires that the building be approved for home purchasing by the VA. Many condos and apartment buildings, including the one I wanted to buy, are not willing to go through the hassle of getting approved by the VA. So, the FHA was my only option.

The FHA loan is a good option for first time home buyers, the downside of FHA loans is that they require you to pay mortgage insurance premiums. The FHA's policies change periodically, but the current policy requires buyers to pay 1.75% of the loan amount, which can get rolled into the loan, plus annual premiums which are 0.45% to 1.05% of the loan amount each year. On my $230,000 condo, the FHA premium was about $230 per month.

If you compare the FHA loan to a traditional loan, these additional premiums can add up to almost an entire percentage point. So, if a traditional mortgage APR is 3.5%, an FHA loan at 3.5% is actually closer to 4.5%. For every $100,000, the difference between 1% (1 point), is about $20,000 over the life of a 30-year mortgage. Because of mortgage insurance premiums, traditional mortgages and VA loans are usually better deals than the FHA.

While the FHA is available to all citizens, the VA is only offered to active-duty service members and vets. Like the FHA, the VA loan also does not require a down payment; however, it does require that borrowers pay a funding fee. For a first-time home buyer with a 0% down payment, the funding fee is 2.3%, and this fee decreases to 1.4% if you can pay a 10% or more down payment. Instead of paying this fee upfront, many borrowers will roll this cost into the mortgage. These fees change periodically, so do your own research if considering an FHA or VA loan.

If you can make a 20% down payment, you can avoid mortgage insurance and funding fees by getting a traditional mortgage. These are usually the best deals, but 20% down is a lot of money. For my $230,000 condo, that would have been $46,000. When making a down payment like that, you need to consider the opportunity cost.

Putting $46,000 towards a 3.5% mortgage is equivalent to investing in an asset with a 3.5% compounding interest rate. Personally, I would prefer to invest in an asset like an S&P 500 mutual fund which averages an 8% return. Therefore, I always try to have a minimum down payment and 30-year mortgage. For me, I'd rather minimize my initial investment and keep monthly payments as low as possible so that I can use the extra money towards retirement savings in my IRA and TSP.

An alternate strategy is to pay off your mortgage as soon as possible. There is certainly a benefit to paying off your mortgage early. This is especially beneficial after retirement since it is useful to reduce living expenses if you have a fixed retirement income. In order to pay off a mortgage early, one strategy is to pay more than the minimum monthly payment each month. Another strategy is to finance your home purchase with a 15-year mortgage instead of a 30-year. As an added benefit, a 15-year fixed mortgage usually has a lower interest rate than a 30-year.

An alternative to the fixed 15-year or 30-year mortgages are adjustable-rate mortgages (ARM). These mortgages are extremely risky and novice investors should avoid them.

I still prefer the 30-year fixed rate mortgage to minimize my monthly payments so that I can invest my extra cost avoidance elsewhere, like my IRA or TSP. Investing that extra money in an IRA and TSP does require discipline, and for an undisciplined person making a big down payment and taking out a 15-year loan instead of a 30-year loan, can be a forcing function to make sure that you are saving money. Even building equity against a 3.5% interest rate is better than not saving money at all. This is one reason why buying a home continues to be one of the best ways for lower income families to get out of poverty.

On a separate note, a few years after you own a home, you may consider refinancing your mortgage. Although I prefer minimum monthly payments, I have never refinanced a home for the purpose of reducing monthly payments. Refinancing a home incurs additional refinancing costs, which usually add up to several thousand dollars.

The only reason that I have ever refinanced a home is to reduce the interest rate on the loan. A general rule of thumb is that you should refinance your mortgage if you can reduce your interest rate by 1% or more. In 2020, I refinanced my third home to reduce my interest rate from 4.25% to 3.0%.

If your home appreciates in value quickly, or if you plan to move and don't want the hassle of renting it, you may consider selling it. In this case, it is important to consider the tax implications of selling your home. Generally, the rule is that you can avoid paying tax on the sale of a home if the home was your primary residence for at least two of the previous five years. As an example, if you sell a home for $100,000 profit, the taxes may be $20,000 to $30,000. If you are within the five-year test, you would be exempt from paying that tax. Fortunately, there is an exception for military members under certain conditions. This exemption extends the five-year limit by an additional ten years. Before you sell your home, you should fully understand the tax implications of that sale.

When I was in grad school, I loved my condo in Nashville. It overlooked dozens of bars, restaurants, and clubs. In the evenings, I could sit on my balcony on the 20th floor and watch the rabble rousers below. On Friday nights, I could tell how much energy was in the city by listening for the *woo girls*.

I don't' really understand the phenomena, but frequently when a group of girls were walking down the street, for example a bachelorette party moving from a restaurant to a night club, they would spontaneously yell out a celebratory "Woooo!"

With my balcony door open, I could pinpoint the location of every group of woo girls. Nashville is the Woo Girl Capital of the World.

Perhaps I enjoyed hearing and laughing at the ideocracy of the howling because it reminded me that despite my divorce, there were plenty of single women in the city. Fortunately, I could shut my thick double-paned balcony door and turn on some Nina Simone when I wanted peace and quiet from the drunken party below.

I loved Nashville. I'm incredibly grateful that the Army sent me to graduate school there. And I am happy that I bought my first home in the city.

When it comes to buying a home, I know some investors that meticulously calculate their initial and future monthly payments, cash flow, depreciation, maintenance, and other costs. While it's important to have a general understanding of these costs, I've never been meticulous about the numbers. This is odd considering that I love data science.

When I bought my Nashville condo, I wasn't big into the numbers because it was very difficult to calculate the risk of buying my Nashville condo. At the time, the economy was still recovering from the recession and prices for homes were near all-time highs. The condo I bought was new and I didn't have a pre-recession price to compare it too, nor was I able to accurately calculate how 25% vacancy in the building affected the price. In a condo of 360 units, 90 properties were for sale, all within a few feet of my property and all with nearly identical features. I had no clue how to calculate those risks, nor did I know how the vacancies would affect rent when I moved in two years. I hoped that the building would fill up before I moved out, but I wasn't certain.

Buying that condo was my largest financial investment up to that point in my life. Before buying the condo, I was anxious and knew that there were risks, but somehow, I felt like I was at the right moment in time and right place in my life to buy the condo.

It's a weird feeling and I can't really explain it. I surely did some analysis but at the end of the day a large part of my decision to buy the condo came down to a gut feeling. In addition to analytical decision making, your gut feeling is an invaluable tool.

My gut feelings have driven many of my investments. Sometimes I get it wrong and sometimes I get it right. I believe that your gut feeling is a skill that you need to train. If you can start training your gut feeling early in life, with small investments, it will help you later in life when you are making large investments.

The decision to buy my Nashville condo worked out well for me. In less than six months, the condo filled up to 100% capacity. When I PCSed, the property value had increased from $230,000 to $270,000. I made $50,000 in equity in less than two years.

Today, I rent out my condo for $2,100 per month. My cash flow is net zero. The rental income barley covers the cost of the mortgage, HOA, and upkeep, but each month I gain about $450 in equity as my mortgage balance gets paid off.

Because of rental property depreciation, I also save thousands of dollars each year in tax deductions. Today in 2021, my mortgage balance is currently $160,000 and my condo is worth over $330,000. My equity in the property is $170,000—*Wooo!*

LET'S RECAP

When buying a home, decide what your objective is. For example: buying place to call home, investing in a property to build equity, or establishing rental property to create positive cash flow. Determining which one is your priority will affect your buying decisions.

Take control of the house hunting process. You have access to almost all of the same property listings as your realtor. Pick which properties you want to visit and then have your realtor schedule showings.

There are benefits to either paying off a mortgage as soon as possible or to minimizing your monthly payments. You should understand the benefits of each and decide which is the best strategy for your financial goals.

It can be difficult to calculate risk for large investment decisions. Even after you do a thorough analysis, you may still need to rely on your gut feeling.

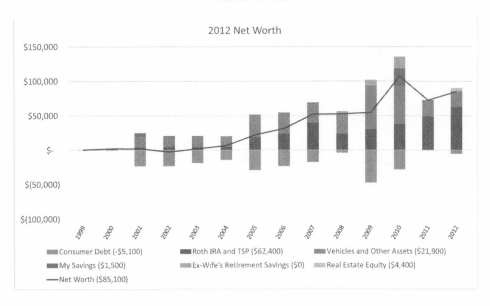

STARTUPS

In grad school, I lived like a king. The Army paid for my tuition and as a newly promoted major I was making over $100,000 a year. As a single bachelor, I could pay my rent and utilities, max out my IRA, start contributing 10% towards my TSP again, and still have thousands of dollars of disposable income each month.

I could eat Hattie B's Hot Chicken for lunch whenever I wanted or bounce between the fine dining restaurants in town. A $30 meal for one, plus a $40 bottle of wine, was a run of the mill Wednesday night whenever I didn't feel like cooking. I was debt free, owned a home, saved about $1,500 each month towards retirement, and was enjoying the bachelor life.

Eventually, I started dating a girl in my condo building. We had an immediate connection. Not only was she a young professional like me, but she was also the only other Black resident in the entire 360-unit condo. While I was happy to date women from any race and was previously married to a White woman, I admit that as an Afro Latino in Nashville I frequently felt like an outsider. My girlfriend and I were outsiders together. She was a beautiful dark caramel skinned Ethiopian American.

Although Nashville is becoming more diversified, it is still predominantly White, especially in higher income areas like downtown. My luxury high rise condo building was even more White than the rest of Nashville. New neighbors in my building frequently look at me suspiciously the first time they saw me enter the lobby of our luxury condo, especially if, God forbid, I was wearing a hoodie. As a Black man, I did not fit Tennessee's normal upper-class professional demographic.

The unfortunate reality is that as my income has increased and as I've moved to more wealthy communities, the number of my Black and Latino neighbors has decreased dramatically. In our condo in Nashville, the number of Black and Latino concierges, security guards, and janitors greatly outnumbered the number of Black and Latino residents. This is a trend that I have become increasingly more aware of and one that repeats itself in cities, suburbs, luxury hotels, first-class flights, and corporations throughout America.

The diversity in the senior ranks of the military is not great, but it is much better than many other areas of American society. As I've grown professionally and personally, I am even more appreciative of the diversity in the military.

My girlfriend was amazing. She was intelligent, gorgeous, and had an amazing sense of humor. On Saturday nights, we loved hanging out on our balconies and making fun of the woo girls below.

Although she could easily be a comedian, she worked in medical sales. Apparently, her sense of humor could also convince doctors and hospitals to buy hundred-thousand-dollar X-Ray machines. She was good at her job and had her shit together. She was beautiful, intelligent, ambitious, and best of all, she wasn't a woo girl. We started dating and soon our relationship got serious.

As the relationship got steamy, we began to spend almost every evening and night together. We would spend a few days in my condo and then a few days in hers. We went back and forth like this, spending about half the month in each other's apartments.

Eventually, I got the idea to rent my condo on Airbnb. I rented my luxury condo for $270 a night. Usually, it rented for about 10 nights a month which, after taxes and fees, was enough to cover my entire mortgage, homeowner's association fees, utilities, and then some. My Airbnb hustle was my first profitable business as an adult. As if I wasn't already living the good life as a recently promoted major, I was also living in a luxury condo for free and had a fine ass girlfriend.

One weekend, I volunteered as a workshop instructor at a STEM conference for high school students. During our lunch break, the event organizer, my Vanderbilt classmate, grabbed me in the hallway and pulled me over to meet another instructor.

"You need to meet my friend Jessica," she told me excitedly, "Jessica has a super cool app doing route planning stuff."

She turned her attention to her friend, "Jessica, he's a pilot in the Army. We worked on an Army project that is super relevant to your app. Ya'll should connect!"

My classmate waved goodbye and bustled off to do some event organizer activities.

I introduced myself, "Hi. Nice to meet you. So, you two are friends?"

"Yeah. We were in undergrad together."

After exchanging a few more introductory pleasantries, I explained that I worked on a route optimization problem for Army aircraft. While I was deployed in Iraq and Afghanistan, one of our most time-consuming tasks in the operations shop was planning for our Blackhawk crews. Every day we received dozens of air mission requests and our planners spent hours manually trying to plan the best flight routes to get everyone to their requested destinations. It was a tedious and time-consuming task. For one of our computer science classes, my classmate and I developed an app to automate this process.

After I explained our research project, I returned to the purpose of the introduction, "Jessica, I heard that you have a super cool app?"

As if on command, Jessica's tone changed and she launched into a pitch that she had probably practiced a few hundred times, "Yes. Our Sh-Opto-Time app allows mall shoppers to optimize their routes, avoid long checkout lines, and save time in shopping malls. When a shopper goes to the mall, they select which stores they want to visit. Then we use real-time geolocation data, artificial intelligence, and predictive analytics to calculate the optimal path through the mall to minimize walking distance and avoid long checkout lines. We are developing a beta version of the app. The potential for ad revenue is incredible. If we can capture just 1% of this market, we will be a billion-dollar company."

"Wow." I tried to process everything she said. If nothing else, I gave her major points for reciting her pitch as if she was a new cadet reciting Schofield's Definition of Discipline.

"That's really interesting. Are you looking for investors?"

"Yes."

"Well, I might be interested in investing if you need some help. Do you have any info that you could send me?"

"Yes, definitely," Jessica replied emphatically, "I'll send you my pitch deck."

A few days later, Jessica sent me her pitch deck and we scheduled a virtual meeting.

It is interesting to note that she hosted the meeting on a new software platform that I previously never heard of. It was easy to use, intuitive, and much better than Skype or any other video conference service I had ever used. The year was 2014 and the app was called Zoom. Jessica was one of the first million users of the app.

Jessica walked me through her pitch deck. She explained her go-to-market strategy and financial predictions. With over 100,000 shopping malls in the United States, and each of those malls having an average of 10 million shoppers per year, she estimated that her market was one trillion shoppers. If only 1% of those visitors used her app, and the app collected a mere 10 cents of ad revenue per mall visit, then her company's annual revenue would be over one billion dollars.

"Wow. That would be something! What size investments are you looking for?" I asked at the end of our conversation.

Jessica replied confidently and well-rehearsed, "During this seed round, we are looking for investments of at least $25,000 each. Our goal is to raise $250,000 the get us to Series A."

"Ok," I replied confidently, "I was thinking about maybe investing about $5,000 but let me think about it and get back to you."

I sounded confident, but I didn't know what she was talking about. Seed Round and Series A were foreign words to me and $25,000 was a lot of money!

I read that 9 out of 10 startups failed. I was looking to potentially invest $5,000 because I rationalized that over the next few years, I would be willing to accept the risk of investing in 10 different companies. A total investment of $50,000 spread out across ten companies would be a good investment if at least one of them had a 20x return or more. If Jessica could grow her business from an idea to a $10 billion dollar company, being one of the first investors could lead to a lot of money.

Over the next two weeks, I educated myself on startup investing. I watched dozens of YouTube videos and read books about startups and investing. Here are some of the resources that I recommend:

"Startup Funding Explained" by The Rest of Us is a short 10-minute YouTube video that does a good job at explaining startup funding.

Additionally, here are some great books that every startup founder or investor should read.

The Lean Start Up by Eric Ries
Zero to One by Peter Theil
Delivering Happiness by Tony Hsieh
The Hard Thing About Hard Things by Ben Horowitz
Shoe Dog by Phil Knight

In addition to being great books about startups, they are also great leadership books. Although I was an officer in the U.S. Army, I like to think that I was an entrepreneur within the larger organization, aka an intrapreneur. Learning about startups and investing has helped shape my leadership style and management decisions.

Most people will never invest in a startup or business, but I've found that as I've gotten older and more of my classmates and friends have ventured into the business world, the opportunities to invest in startups and small businesses has also increased. A few times a year, I have friends or colleagues invite me to invest in different real estate syndicates, new venture capital funds, or startups.

Many startup investment opportunities require you to be an accredited investor. An accredited investor is generally someone that has an annual income greater than $200,000 and a net worth greater than $1 million. Although most sophisticated high-risk investments require you to be accredited, I've found that there are still many startup investment opportunities for non-accredited investors. This is especially true in the very early stages of a startup that are raising money from friends and family.

As with all investments, investing in a business has a certain degree of uncertainty. Investing in small businesses has some of the greatest number of potential rewards, but also the greatest amount of risk.

I'm involved in a few different businesses now, including some of my own. I am certainly not an expert in business investing, but here some questions that you should ask yourself before you decide to invest in a business.

1. Can you afford to lose it all?

If you invest in a small business or startup, you should prepare to lose all your money. In fact, after you make an investment, you should mentally write off that investment as a loss. You definitely need to have faith that a business will succeed, but similar to playing the lottery, don't realistically expect to make any money.

2. Do you have faith in the founders?

Many novice investors focus most of their energy into analyzing a business financial projections or technology. The most successful companies usually experience a series of evolutions, changes, and 180-degree turns before they succeeded. These pivots are nearly certain with startups, and revenue projections rarely come into fruition as predicted—Jessica's billion dollar projection was a pipe dream.

Knowing that the business model, technology, and financial projections will change, then the most consistent aspect of a business becomes the founders. Before investing in a business, you need to have faith in the founders and believe that they will stick with the business against all odds, that they are smart enough and humble enough to learn and pivot when needed, and that they won't screw you over the moment they can.

3. What do you bring to the table?

If you ever decide to invest in a business, you become part owner of that business. You become responsible for the business's success. The role that you have in the business will depend on your agreement with the founder. Even if you have a limited role, you can still help the founder team be successful by providing mentorship, business connections, professional services, word of mouth marketing, and moral support.

While a small $5,000 investment does not give you the right to become a board member, most founders will welcome additional help and support from their investors. Investing in a small business is frequently just as much of an emotional and professional investment as it is a financial investment. You can help an investor prepare pitch decks, test beta products, or introduce founders to the West Point alumni network.

As an Army officer, it is against regulations to use your official position for personal profit, so you should avoid companies that sell exclusively to the military or that operate in sectors related to your duty, but there are plenty of non-military focused companies that could benefit from your expertise. If there is an ethical concern about investing in a company, you should get an opinion from your Staff Jude Advocate.

4. How will you make a profit?

One of the most important questions, and frequently the hardest to answer is about the exit strategy, e.g. how you plan to make money from the investment. There are many different types of exit strategies. For example, a company can agree to pay future dividends, you may hope to get bought out if the company gets acquired, or you can sell your shares if the company were to ever have an initial public offering (IPO).

In terms of tech startups, the most sought-after exit strategy is the IPO. The videos and books I mentioned earlier cover the process in more detail but in summary the tech start up process goes like this... The startup lifecycle begins when a founder has a great idea and begins developing it. At this point, the founder owns 100% of the company. Frequently, they will begin investing their own money into growing the company or idea.

Eventually the founder needs more money to scale, perhaps to hire engineers or buy equipment. The founder issues equity, or an agreement for future equity, to cover these costs. A founder may ask for investments from her friends and family which is when most novice investors can invest in a startup.

If the company continues to grow, it may have a series of seed rounds, series A, B, C, or more. Each of these subsequent investment rounds gets larger and larger until, if the company does well, it goes public either through an IPO or through an acquisition by a larger company.

Once a company is public, then shareholders can sell their shares in the stock market to recover their initial investment, or investors can get bought out during an acquisition. This entire process leading to a profitable exit strategy can take years, decades, or never.

There are countless other strategies for investing in businesses. Whether investing in a tech startup, real estate syndicate, or local coin laundry shop, the key is to have a goal for how and when you hope to get profit from your investment.

5. How does the investment support your personal and professional goals?

You will have more personal satisfaction as an investor if your investments support your personal and professional goals. Of course, most of us have a goal to make a lot of money, but ideally your business investments should support your other values, beliefs, and long-term professional goals. For example, you may take pride in supporting Black or veteran owned businesses, you may want to support businesses that support environmental conservation, or if you are a pilot, you may want to invest in the aerospace industry. Whatever your goals are, you will be a better investor if your business investments align with them.

Ultimately, I turned down Jessica's opportunity. I thought the idea was great, but I did not see a path to user adoption. I didn't think that most mall shoppers cared how long checkout lines were or were eager to optimize their travel path. I also didn't know Jessica well enough to trust her success.

Since grad school, I've had a few other small business investment opportunities. Here are a few examples.

I had a West Point classmate approach me and ask if I wanted to invest in his company that made custom football gloves for local school teams. With so much competition from big companies like Nike and ADIDAS, I didn't think that he would ever be able to reach an IPO. My probability of a successful exit was too low, so I turned it down. The company has been extraordinarily successful, and I am delighted to see his success.

I had another classmate that was looking for investors to help fund his startup which sought to use under water drones to inspect ship hulls. His idea sounded promising, but he still had a corporate job at Ford, and I didn't trust that he was willing to take the required personal and financial risk to make the startup successful. It seemed like he was willing to risk other people's money, but not any of his own. So, I passed on his startup. He gave up on his business idea shortly after.

Finally, I became friends with an Air Force veteran who was using drones to collect high resolution 3D imagery of the United States, much higher resolution than Google Earth. He had already been working on the company for two years and had a prototype. I thought that my experience as an Aviator and systems engineer could potentially benefit him. Throughout my master's degree program, I also made connections with a few other drone companies which I thought may be useful to him. I also saw a huge potential market for his product and was really interested in his development and operations processes. After meeting a few times and sharing a few beers, I invested in his company.

It was a small investment, only $5,000 of a total $250,000 he raised so far. His valuation was $3 million. $5,000 of $250,000 may not seem like a lot, but it helped him cover his development costs and extend his runway during a critical phase of his business's growth.

I never expect to see that money again, but watching his company grow and supporting him when I can has been an immensely rewarding experience. Investing in a company where I have a personal relationship with the founder is more intrinsically rewarding than my stock market investments. Rarely in investing, can you really help someone chase after their dreams in a tangible way. If nothing else, I enjoy being a cheerleader as I watch my friend's company grow.

If you ever have a good opportunity to invest in a small business, I strongly encourage you give it a try with a small investment (after due diligence of course, and preferably with money that you are willing to lose).

Investing in my friends' company has been exciting. Not only do I hope that the startup will become successful and make us a lot of money, but I have also gained more perspective on the broader startup ecosystem and stock market. Investing in startups is risky but can be very rewarding both financially and otherwise.

LET'S RECAP

Investing in startups and small businesses can be extremely risky but can have 10x to 100x returns.

Before investing in a high-risk startup or business, consider whether you are comfortable losing your investment, how much faith you have in the founders, what you can contribute to the team, your exit strategy, and your personal goals.

Investing in a small business is a great opportunity to learn about startups and to be part of something truly special.

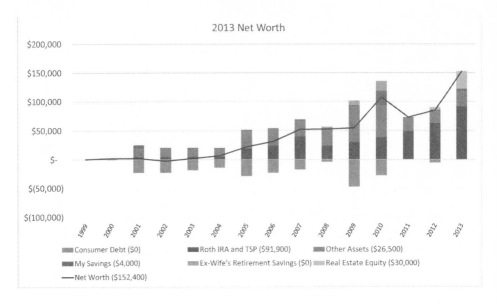

STOCKS

After grad school, I headed to Fort Leavenworth, Kansas to serve in a TRADOC Capability Management office. The TCM job opened my eyes to the business side of the Army. At the company and battalion levels, it is easy to complain about seemingly stupid Pentagon decisions like the gray digital camouflage pattern or the decision to retire the OH-58D helicopter. In my new role, I got higher-level insight into how and why many Army wide decisions were made.

Decisions frequently involve dozens of different influential stake holders like general officers, operational commanders, program offices, industry partners, congress, and of course, the soldiers in the field. Government sausage making is an interesting process and working in the TCM office really gave me insight into how the government and Army works at the highest levels.

While at Leavenworth, I also began investing more seriously. I bought a second house using a VA loan and began trading stocks more regularly. I certainly was not a day trader, but I made a handful of trades per month in my Roth IRA account, which was up to about $65,000 in value. After looking back at the decline of my GE stock over a decade, I decided that I should probably keep better tabs on my portfolio performance to identify and pull out of a declining position earlier. I was also eager to find another multi-bagger like Lockheed.

I should warn you that if you decide to trade in stocks, the odds are against you. I've heard that most retail investors perform worse than the S&P 500 or Dow Jones Industrial Average. If you are considering trading individual stocks, think long and hard about your goals and risk tolerance. There is a good chance that you would have a better ROI if you invested in a mutual fund or broad market Exchange Traded Funds (ETFs) like the Vanguard VFINX or the SPY which track the S&P 500.

If you want a narrower focus than the S&P 500, you could alternatively invest in specialty ETFs. There are a wide variety of ETFs that you can invest in. For example, ARKK invests in high growth technology companies, DRIV invests in autonomous and electric vehicle technology, HDV tracks high-dividend companies, the QQQ invests in the NASDAQ 100, and YOLO invests in the marijuana industry. You can learn more about these funds by searching for their tickers on Yahoo Finance or your favorite financial website. Many of these ETFs historically out-perform the S&P 500 and are great options if you want a more focused portfolio than the broader S&P 500 or Down Jones Industrial Average.

Although I'm a big fan of mutual funds and ETFs, I've had moderate success in trading stocks. Admittedly, I also enjoy trading stocks more than ETFs or other investments. Buying deep value stocks and then holding them for an extended period of time continues to be one of my most rewarding trading strategies.

It's important to note that although I talk a lot about my favorite stocks and crypto on social media and in this book, the truth is that most of my wealth is in my lower risk TSP mutual funds, real estate, and ETFs. Trading individual stocks can be risky. If you trade stocks, and if you expand to more complex trading strategies, tread lightly otherwise you may lose a lot of money.

I learned most of my stock trading experience through failures, losing tens of thousands of dollars along the way. If you begin trading stocks, I hope that your lessons cost less than mine.

For investors who are just beginning to trade stocks, my recommendation is to begin by opening up a brokerage account. E*TRADE, Schwab, Ameritrade, and Webull are some brokerage services but there are many others.

I'm a big fan of trading stocks within a Roth IRA, but I recommend practicing trading techniques in a non-Roth IRA account first. If you want to start trading, open a trading account and make an initial deposit even before you decide where to invest it.

Most first-time investors should start with an initial investment that makes them feel a little uncomfortable, but not so much that losing the investment would be very painful. I've known many young professionals who began trading with an amount between $2,000 to $5,000.

Before placing a trade, I recommend that investors pick a handful of companies they like and then spend a few weeks conducting due diligence on those companies. Read quarterly earnings reports, check out the company website, follow the company's CEO on Twitter, and add the company to a watch list. I am a particular fan of the watchlist features on the free version of Yahoo Finance. Yahoo provides a lot of different information about companies all in one place to include news, stock price fundamentals, company financials, and charts, but there are certainly many other similar services on the web.

After you spend a few weeks conducting due diligence, then my next recommendation is to pick a few of your favorite stocks and buy them. For first time investors, one of the primary factors that I recommend they consider is whether or not they think the companies they select will continue to grow for the next five to ten years. This timeline is important, because I recommend first-time investors buy-and-hold their initial stocks for a few years.

As an added benefit of holding stocks for over a year, long term investments are usually taxed at the lower capital gains tax rate (currently 20% or less) instead of the higher short-term gains which are usually taxed at your higher income tax rate. In a Roth IRA account, where gains are not taxed, the difference is insignificant, but in a regular brokerage account, the difference between capital gains and short-term gains can be as high as 15% or more.

It's important to note that at the time of writing this, politicians have proposed to increase the capital gains tax. If the capital gains tax rates increases, the difference between short and long term investments may become negligible. Even if the capital gains tax rates increases during this administration, I suspect that it will decrease again in 5 to 10 years. Tax rates are an important consideration when making investment decisions.

Before investors begin more frequent trading, it's important to learn how a stock performs over an extended period of time, not only by reviewing historical information, but by actually having your own money on the line. An important aspect of investing is learning how stocks behave, but more importantly, investors need to learn their own emotional reactions to the up and down fluctuations of stock prices.

Learning my own behavior patterns has been a key aspect of my financial growth. During my growth as an investor, I've made hundreds of different stock purchases, too many to recall all of them, but here are a few of the biggest ones which shaped my stock trading strategy.

To begin, one of my biggest investments early in my career was in Facebook. In 2012 when Facebook IPOed, I bought $8,000 worth of FB at $45 per share.

Compared to my usually investments of $1,000 to $2,000, it was significantly larger than any of my previous stock purchases.

Long before their IPO, I was a big fan of Facebook. I signed up for Facebook around 2004 when it was still mostly used by college students or recent college grads. Over the next few years, it grew in popularity and it really helped me connect with friends and family members back home during my combat deployments. Mark Zuckerberg wanted to connect the world on Facebook, and I really believed that he would. I imagined a future where everyone had a Facebook account.

Despite my conviction, for the next three months after their IPO, Facebook seemed to fail miserably. Everyone complained that the stock was incredibly overpriced. More concerning than that was that Facebook couldn't seem to make any revenue. The financial news channels ripped on Facebook nonstop. Companies were not spending money on Facebook ads and it seemed like Facebook would eventually go the direction of Myspace. The stock was falling steadily, and it looked like there was no end to the blood bath. I was afraid I made mistake by investing in Facebook.

Three months after IPO, the stock price was approaching $20. I was afraid that it would pass through $20 and continue to decline to $10 or less. Before it could go below $20, I sold all my shares at $22 for a 50% loss, or $4,000.

I was partially correct; the stock did continue to decline. The following month, it dropped to $18. For a moment I celebrated my wise decision to cut my losses. Of course, $18 was the lowest the stock ever got. A month after I sold, it began a steady and relentless uphill climb to today's highs of $300 per share, an average rate of return of more than 20% per year. If I would have held on instead of selling, my initial investment of $8,000 would be worth $50,000. If instead of selling at $22, I doubled down and bought another $8,000, then my investment would be worth $150,000. Instead, I lost $4,000.

Selling Facebook was one of my biggest mistakes because deep in my heart I knew that the company would be successful. The user base was growing by leaps and bounds. The company grew from an extremely loyal fan base and was a favorite of everyone, including grandmothers, teeny boppers, and local businesses. And, I was a big fan of Mark Zuckerberg's vision for Facebook's future. Sure, Facebook struggled to make ad revenue, but I should have known that with such a huge growth rate, they would have figured out a way to make money.

Instead of trusting my own assessment, I listened to entertainers like Jim Cramer. The news has an incredibly strong ability to prey upon our emotions, and I gave into those emotions despite my better judgement.

Controlling my emotions when reading or watching the news has been one of the most important lessons I learned from that experience. It also continues to be one of my most difficult challenges. It is incredibly difficult to hold on to a stock when everyone is telling you that it's time to sell. The ability to make a good call despite public opinion has led to some of my most lucrative investments. This lesson helped me significantly a few years later when I invested in Tesla.

When I was at the TCM office, I had to sell my Lockheed stock. We expected Lockheed to bid on an upcoming contract that I was involved with. In the big picture, I owned a miniscule fraction of Lockheed. I would never make a decision while on duty for a personal profit motive, nor did I expect that any work I was doing would impact Lockheed's stock price. Yet, to be completely free of any conflicts of interest, I sold my LMT stock.

If you are ever in a role that deals with contract decision making, you may be required to submit an OGE 450 financial declaration form to your legal office. If you are in such a role, your office's lawyer will probably make sure that you declare your investments, and if there is a conflict of interest, your lawyer will probably let you know. Still, if you are ever in an office that makes decisions about government contracts, it is your responsibility to avoid or report any potential conflicts of interests between your personal financial investments and professional duties. Failure to do so can result in UCMJ legal actions or jail time.

Most junior officers in operational units will never need to worry about stuff like this, but senior officers in Department of the Army staff positions, capability or requirement management offices, the Acquisition Corps, and the new Army Future's Command Cross-Functional Teams may run into these issues. If ever in doubt, talk to your Staff Judge Advocate.

I bought 40 shares of LMT in 1999 for about $22 per share and sold in 2014 for $195 per share. I took my profit and bought 50 shares of Tesla (TSLA) for about $193 per share, an investment of about $10,000.

In 2014, Tesla was still an up-and-coming company. Tesla cars were still a luxury vehicle and charging stations were rare outside of California. For having such a small production, Tesla stock was grossly overvalued by industry standards. Most analysist expected Tesla to go bankrupt or get acquired by a larger company like Apple. Still, I thought Elon Musk had a great idea and I loved the idea of self-driving cars. Despite repeated negative reviews of the company, I stood by my investment decision.

For about five years, the stock price barely increased, and then from 2018 to 2020 it surged. In 2020, the stock split 5-for-1 and later was added to the S&P 500. If I held on to my original 50 shares of TSLA, my investment would have turned into 250 shares at $850 each. My $10,000 investment would be worth $212,000.

In actuality, I sold most of my shares of TSLA and locked in my profit as the stock price skyrocketed. I still own about 50 shares post-split. Although I didn't have $200,000 profit, I still earned over a $100,000 profit. I was happy to stand by Elon Musk when most of the financial industry doubted him and I saw a healthy profit in return.

On the flip side, I've also invested in companies that I did not believe in but which promised a quick return. For example, when the National Bank of Greece (NBG) began to fail, I invested in it, not because I knew anything about the Bank or Greece, but instead because I imagined that the Greek government or European Union would bailout the bank similar to how the U.S. government bailed out our financial institutions in 2008. I hoped that I could make a quick 50% on the rebound. The bailout never happened, and the National Bank of Greece collapsed taking all of my initial $5,000 investment with it.

Similarly, in 2016 when oil prices dropped from $100 per barrel to $50 per barrel, I invested in an oil drilling company stock. At the time, I was already well invested in Elon Musk's dream of an electric vehicle future. I thought oil companies were greedy, environment destroying, soulless corporations. Despite my beliefs, I bought stock in an oil company because everyone expected oil to return to $100 per barrel. Oil never recovered to $100 and the company I invested in went bankrupt along with $3,000 of my investment.

These experiences taught me that the most valuable strategy in investing is to have faith and conviction in the company you are investing in. My best investments have always been in the companies whose fundamental mission and values I believed in, and my worst investments have been when I focused only on profit opportunities.

If you have conviction in the company, then you will stick with them through the ups and downs. If you focus on the company, and not the promise of profit, you will be more likely to weather bad news and negative press coverage. You need to hold on to good investments with *diamond hands*.

In contrasts, if you are primarily focused on making profit, you will probably sell the moment things start looking bad. The best companies make it through these temporary storms and sail to all-time highs. If you have diamond hands, not only will you be more likely to hold your position through the storms, but you will also be more inclined to double down and buy more when things look worst. This can be a very lucrative strategy, but can be extremely stressful if you don't confidently believe in the companies you are investing in.

To build that kind of trust in a company, one of the strategies I've found useful is to conduct research beyond superficial news reports and social media. Every company files periodic paperwork with the SEC. For example, before an IPO, a company is required to file a S-1 Investment Prospectus. These documents are available to the public and usually include tons of great information about the company, revenue, and even executive salaries.

Another great resource is quarterly earning calls. Most companies are required to publish their quarterly earnings and have quarterly conference calls. Anyone can dial into these calls. They can be a little boring, but they contain great information about company performance and priority projects. In an age with so much fake news, where everyone is a critic, these resources come straight from the company. Although they are always biased in favor of the company, they at least allow you to develop your own opinions and beliefs instead of relying on news hosts or YouTubers who are predominantly entertainers and not financial analysts.

In terms of investing, I also think that there is something to be said about ethics and values. Many investors disagree with me about this, but I think that you can, and should, invest ethically based upon your values.

I came to this realization after losing money on the oil company. Big oil companies are incentivized to continue the oil economy, which I believe is bad for the environment. Despite this belief, I gave my money to a big oil company because I placed profit ahead of my values. I lost thousands of dollars but in doing so I promised myself that I would never again invest in a company whose foundational purpose I disagreed with.

Today, I apply the same value-based investing criteria to China based companies. Our nation is in a power competition with China. China has historically stolen American intellectual property, they violate human rights, and their commercial industry supports their communist regime. By Chinese law, every company in China is required to "support and cooperate in national intelligence work." Furthermore, private companies in China are required to have internal communist party committees. Investing in these companies is directly corelated to supporting the communist party.

More egregious is that when U.S. investors buy stocks in Chinese companies listed in U.S. exchanges, they are not actually buying any ownership or voting rights in these companies. Instead, they are buying stock in powerless shell corporations in places like the Cayman Islands. These shell corporations have high risk of Chinese government interference and insider trading.

When I began trading more regularly, I originally invested in Chinese companies like Baidu (similar to Google) and Alibaba (similar to Amazon), but the more I thought about it, the more I realized that these were bad investments for the reasons I just listed. I sold my investments in those companies and I no longer invest in Chinese-based companies.

Ethical investing is not always cut and dry. There are some companies like Palantir that refuse to do business with China, but most American companies like Apple and Google have a significant portion of their business in China. It is certainly difficult to be an ethical investor, but at a minimum I believe that companies with guidons in the United States are generally more ethical investments than companies headquartered in Beijing. I know that this is a gray area, but I try to make value-based investments.

Whether you are against China, big oil, big pharma, gun manufacturers, or whatever else, I recommend that you invest based on your own values. It is a challenge, but if you have good intentions, value-based investing is possible.

When it comes to stocks, another strategy I use is to concentrate in a market sector. One of the lessons I learned while investing is that: The fastest way to build wealth is to invest in a concentrated portfolio (this is also the fastest way to lose wealth).

Instead of spreading my stock investments across a hundred stocks, I instead focus on ten to twenty stocks, most within the same sector. At any given time, I have thirty to fifty companies that I monitor, and of those I invest in the ten to twenty most promising.

Currently, I am particularly focused on companies that have synergy with artificial intelligence. I'm invested in about ten to fifteen companies in this sector, which account for about 90% of my overall stock portfolio. From low risk to high risk, some of the current companies in my personal artificial intelligence mutual fund are as follows.

Amazon (AMZN), cloud computing

Nvidia (NVDA), graphics cards

Taiwan Semiconductor Manufacturing (TSM), semiconductors

Advanced Micron Devices (AMD), computer chips

Tesla (TSLA), self-driving cars

Snowflake (SNOW), data management

SalesForce (CRM), business intelligence

UpStart, (UPST), lending

Schrödinger (SDGR), pharmaceuticals

AbCellera, (ABCL), pharmaceuticals

Cripser (CRSP), gene editing

C3 AI, (AI), AI systems

I post periodic updates about my investments and my strategies on Twitter. If you want to see how my investment are doing or if you have any questions, connect with me on Twitter @TheCadetX.

As I learned with Lockheed, Tesla, and Facebook, picking a few superstar companies and then sticking with them for about five years, is a financially rewarding strategy. By focusing on one sector, or one technology aspect, I can educate myself much deeper than I would be able to if I was spread out across different industries. Conversely, I've lost the most money when I chased short-term trends, spread my investments too thin, or invested in sectors that I knew little about.

I get excited about artificial intelligence, but there are similar sectors that are equally promising. For example, you could set up a portfolio that focusses on marijuana stocks, cryptocurrency, self-driving cars, the defense industry, cyber security, green energy, or companies that appeal to consumers. I frequently joke with my wife that she should invest in *The Basic Becky Index*: Apple (AAPL), Facebook (FB), Honest Company (HNST), Lululemon (LULU), Louis Vuitton (LVMUY), Netflix (NFLX), Pinterest (PINS), Planet Fitness (PLNT), Peloton (PTON), Starbucks (SBUX), Target (TGT), and Ulta Beauty (ULTA).

Whichever sector or companies you favor, I recommend that you focus in one area that excites you and then concentrate there. Pick companies that you confidently think will grow and thrive for the next five to ten years. For new investors, I recommend avoiding penny stocks (usually listed as over-the-counter securities or OTC) and instead focus on companies in the Dow Jones Industrial Average, S&P 500, or NASDAQ. If you are a first-time investor, begin with two or three companies and then build your portfolio from there until you have about ten to twenty companies in your portfolio.

You can still diversify your risk within that sector, but by concentrating your portfolio and then going all in on those ten to twenty companies, you will be more likely to weather the storms and more likely to pick a winner. If you want lower risk, you can diversify your portfolio with more stocks.

Historically, I've found that the Pareto Principle repeats itself in stock investing. 20% of my stock investments usually account for 80% of my profits. For every ten companies I invest in, most will perform mediocre, but one or two companies will soar and account for most of my profits.

I take risk in my concentrated stock portfolios because I have diversified investments in my TSP mutual funds, real estate, and other investments. Investing is a continuous risk assessment process.

LET'S RECAP

For investing in stocks, listening solely to news reports and social media can cause you to make emotional decisions which can be very costly mistakes.

The best way to avoid emotional mistakes in stock trading is to invest in companies that you have strong convictions about after conducting due diligence and market research.

Company SEC filings and quarterly earnings conference calls are great resources to learn about companies you are interested in.

The fastest way to get rich is to invest in a concentrated portfolio. This is also the fastest way to lose money, so be cautious.

STOCKS

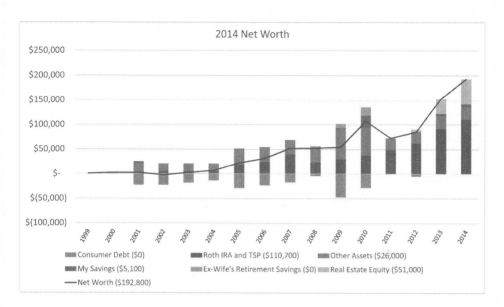

RENTAL PROPERTIES

A year after moving to Fort Leavenworth, my girlfriend and I got engaged. This time instead of spending a fortune on a real diamond, I bought a synthetic moissanite stone instead. A few days after the engagement when I told her it wasn't a real diamond, she was happy that I was able to save a few thousand dollars by buying a synthetic stone. It was a beautiful ring and none of our friends or family could tell that it was not a real diamond.

She still had her sales job based out of Nashville but visited me in Kansas City about once a month.

One particular weekend, my fiancé and I had plans to meet up with friends in Kansas City for brunch. Before we left the house, I got a phone call. It was a potential new tenant that saw my Nashville condo earlier in the week.

"Hello... I got the money. Can I move in today? I just emailed you the signed lease. It'd be really great if I could move in today."

My realtor showed him the rental property earlier in the week. I knew he was interested in the property and we completed a background check, but I was not expecting this call on a Sunday morning.

I was still surprised and replied, "Um, ok. Give me a minute and let me see if I can have someone meet you."

My realtor was out of town for the weekend. I called a friend of mine who lived in a nearby building in Nashville. I arranged for them to meet up later that day so that she could collect the rental payment and security deposit checks and then turn over the keys to him. It was a simple hand over.

Later that day, my fiancé and I met our Kansas City friends for brunch. We were enjoying our bottomless mimosas when my Nashville friend called me, "I have a little bit of a problem."

"Oooh Kay," I replied. "What is it?"

"Jeremy brought all cash. He has $4,500 in ten and twenty dollar bills."

I shook my head, "What?"

My friend was a short and skinny 110 lbs girl. My potential tenant was a 6' 6" 250 lbs ex-linebacker. A few years earlier, he played ball for Vanderbilt but never made it to the pros. According to his background check, he owned a knockoff "Hottie Bee's" chicken wing spot in the ghetto. Showing up with $4,500 in small bills made me suspicious. I didn't want to put my friend in a position where she could get swindled by this guy or potentially robbed as soon as she exited the building. I wasn't happy with the way this was going. I previously told the tenant that the rent and security deposit had to be paid by cashier's check but he obviously ignored me.

Due to problems getting approved to lease the property, the condo had been vacant for three months. After paying two mortgages for that long, I was eager to get someone into the property. I guess cash was the next best thing to a cashier's check.

I told her, "How about this, let Jeremy hold the money. Bank of America should be open. It's a block away. If you're comfortable with it, I'll tell Jeremy to walk with you to the bank and he can deposit the money there. I'll text you guys my account number. Once it's deposited, you can give him the keys. How does that sound?"

"Ok," my baffled friend replied, "I can do that."

Over the next year, I looked back at that day as a series of red flags that should have warned me. Every other month, Jeremy was late with his rent. At one point he stopped paying it for two months. I had to sign my fiancé power of attorney so that she could initiate eviction proceedings with the court. After he received his first court notice, he paid up.

Three months later, he stopped paying rent again. After the second late notice, we began the long eviction process again. In all, it took about three months to evict him. I hired the sheriff and moving company to move all his shit to the curb. He finally moved out on his own accord after I texted him, "The sheriff is coming on Tuesday to evict you. They will place all your property outside near the dumpster."

After he left, I had to get a lighting fixture replaced, the holes from his TV mount patched, and the walls repainted—he painted the entire bedroom a disgusting navy blue. I kept all his $2250 security deposit, but it was not nearly enough to cover the three months of unpaid rent and damages. I could have taken him to court to collect the rest, but honestly, it wasn't worth the headache or time. Since I was living in Kansas and not Nashville, I would have needed to hire a lawyer to represent me remotely. Even if I won in court, the case would have probably gone to collections. After the lawyer and other fees, I would have been lucky to get two thousand dollars after a process that would have taken months. It was not worth the headache to me.

I would say that Jeremy was my worse tenant, but the reason that I had trouble getting approved to lease the property to him was because the previous tenant assaulted a police officer, with a 10" kitchen knife. She attacked her boyfriend, ran through the hallways naked, attacked the police officers, and resisted arrest. The police officers eventually sedated her and carried her away on a stretcher. I suspect that she was on some hardcore drugs. After that, the HOA would not let me rent my property without a full review by the homeowner board.

Over the years, I've had a few issues with tenants. For example, my tenants have received plenty of noise violations, complaints about the smell of weed coming from their balcony, and I had one tenant take a shit in the community pool at 2 am—caught on video. Still, the tenant who assaulted the police and then the tenant who paid his deposit in strip club money were the worst. After I kicked out Jeremy, I considered selling all my properties and never owning a rental ever again.

Everyone loves the idea of a rental property with positive cash flow. It's great if a rental check shows up in your bank account, on time, month after month, year after year. Easy money, right?

It doesn't always happen like that. If you are a landlord long enough, you will eventually have a bad tenant. Even if you have perfect tenants, you will eventually need to replace an air conditioner system, a roof, or another major appliance. Dealing with these issues can be extremely frustrating, especially if you are living on the other side of the country or deployed.

Being a landlord is a job. Sometimes, it requires a lot of work (for example if you need to evict a tenant) and other times it can be minimal work for years at a time. Regardless, it's still a job and a business. It requires a strategy, planning, answering late night calls when a pipe bursts, replacing refrigerators when they stop working, and dealing with angry neighbors when your tenants throw a block party that lasts until 4 am.

To make matters worse, if the property sits vacant for any period, or if you have a squatter that you are trying to evict, you can potentially have months of lost revenue. A property that is vacant for three months could quickly negate three years' worth of positive cash flow. It is awfully difficult for many property owners to adopt this job and business owner mentality. Too often, they think that renting a property will be easy money, when it frequently is not.

Along those lines, another challenge that property owners have is in letting go of their emotional attachment to their previous home. Many homeowners still feel like a tenant is renting out "their home." It is hard to emotionally detach from a property that you lived in for years and to begin treating the management of that property as a business.

Owning rental properties requires a cold and calculated approach, factoring in the mortgage payments, taxes, operating costs, maintenance, principal down payment, market growth, and tax deductions. Positive cash flow is one of the most common goals of landlords, but equity growth and tax deductions are two other benefits that landlords must factor in to determine if the trouble of being a landlord is worth the investment.

Many landlords do not evaluate the *total owner benefits* of owning a rental property. Instead, they only look at the cash flow and compare it to the headaches they have. For these reasons, many landlords give up after one or two bad experiences. I certainly considered giving up after my "shitty" tenant. After two bad tenants, I could have sold my Nashville condo and walked away with $130,000 in profit. The hassle to manage the property didn't seem worth it to me.

That was about five years ago. Fortunately, I kept the condo and the tenants I've had since then have been great. In those five years, the equity of my property has increased from $130,000 to $180,000. The cost of operating my property management business and property depreciation actually result in a net tax deduction each year, meaning that I actually save money each year on my taxes.

Although I own three properties now, all homes that I lived in at one point or another, I have a few friends who take a completely different approach. One of my mentors for example, began purchasing homes when he was a lieutenant at Fort Hood. While I purchased my homes primarily for the purpose of building equity, he purchased his homes for the purpose of cash flow.

He began buying cheap, three-bedroom single family homes in and around Killeen, TX. Each home usually cost between $40,000 and $75,000. It didn't make a difference if they were in the bad part of town. He'd buy them, clean them up with new floors and paint, and then rent them out. For him, cash flow was king.

Before each purchase, he would meticulously calculate the home value, investment cost required to clean it up, and then estimate the monthly rental income and expenses. The cash flow each month was the bottom line. By the time he was a senior captain, he owned five properties.

Eventually, my mentor left Fort Hood and hired his father to help him manage the rental properties. It helped that his father was also a handyman and could assist with any required repairs or remodeling.

After his fifth house or so, he began doing complex financing. For example, he would take out a loan against his previous five properties to buy the sixth. Or he would bulk finance three new properties at a time.

Frequently, he bought properties sight unseen. If a listing popped up for a three-bedroom house for $50,000, he'd buy it. It didn't make a difference if the foundation was cracked or if it was previously a crack house. If it had four walls, a roof, and three bedrooms, it was his. He would buy the homes, and then send in his father to tile the floors, fix the walls, and replace any appliances or other items.

The homes weren't as sexy as on the show *Fixer-Upper*. Purchasing homes was a simple numbers game for him. Although many homes were in the ghetto, his investment into the homes helped a lot of people live in nice simple homes instead of the slums that are so prevalent in some parts of our nation.

There are certainly risks associated with owning a lot of properties. For example, he would have a difficult time finding new tenants if the Army decided to downsize Fort Hood, which is unlikely, but still a concern. Fortunately, the recession didn't hurt him because the demand for low-income housing remained consistent throughout 2008.

Another risk in managing rental properties is the risk of getting sued. Getting sued is probably the least likely event to occur but can be the most catastrophic. If a tenant gets injured because of your negligence as a landlord, they could sue you for millions of dollars. For this reason, insurance is utterly important. I have rental property insurance and umbrella insurance for added protection. I also require my tenants to have their own renter's insurance.

As an extra layer of protection, I know many people that form Limited Liability Companies (LLCs) for property management. By forming an LLC to manage your rental properties, and by properly structuring it with bylaws and separate bank accounts, a landlord can limit their personal liability in the event of a lawsuit. If you own multiple properties, I recommend you contact a lawyer to learn how an LLC or multiple LLCs can help limit your personal liability.

Buying and managing multiple properties is certainly a time-consuming task. Remotely managing properties is a particular challenge for military members who PCS every two to three years. Property management companies are expensive and rarely perform as well as you expect they would. The most successful landlords I've known have always been the ones who homestead in a geographic area for most of their career, or who, like my mentor, have a family member or friend in the area to help manage the properties.

My mentor retired after a 20-year Army career and now lives in Salt Lake City, UT. Today, he owns FORTY-FIVE homes in and around Fort Hood. He rents each for $600 to $900 per month. After his expenses and paying his father and contractors, his take home income is $15,000 per month. He retired as an LTC with a pension of about $65,000 per year. On top of that, he has a full-time corporate job making about $200,000 per year, plus another $50,000 a year in bonuses. In sum, he makes about $500,000 per year between his job, pension, and rental properties. His profitable real estate empire all started because he took a little risk as a lieutenant and bought his first home. Owning 45 rental properties certainly isn't for everyone, but if you want to build wealth, and understand the risk and work required, real estate is a great option.

LET'S RECAP

Being a landlord is a job. The amount of work required will ebb and flow. If you are not mentally prepared to do the job, it can be very stressful.

When evaluating costs and benefits of owning rental properties, you must consider the cash flow, growth in equity value, and tax benefits as compared to the intangible costs of your time and energy.

Owning rental properties has its challenges, but if you want to build wealth and understand the risk and work required, real estate can be a great investment opportunity.

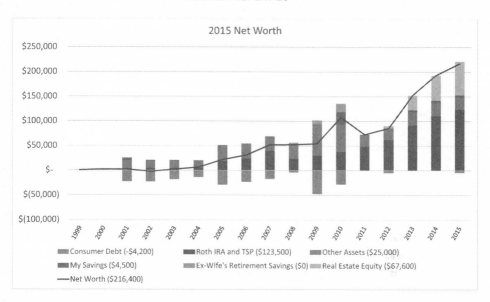

2015 - 2016

MARRIAGE

"Your chick sells medical devices. She's making bank!" my fraternity brother said as he marked his ball on the green, "I ain't never getting married, but if I did, I'd marry a chick like that."

My friends and I were on our fraternity's annual golf trip. This year, we were in the Dominican Republic.

I lined up for my put. My buddies paused while I tapped my ball towards the cup. The ball rolled across the green, curved six inches right of the hole, and then continued rolling down the hill into the fringe.

My wife did have a good job in sales. Her base salary was about $100,000 which was comparable to mine at the time, but she usually made another $50,000 per year in bonuses and commissions.

"Rob's wife is making that money too," I said as I pointed my putter towards my other frat brother who was lining up for his put.

"She's a lawyer and owns her own business. You know she's making that chedda."

"We doing a'ight," Rob said as he sank his put, "Congrats by the way on the wedding man. If I weren't deployed, I would have made it."

"Thanks man," I replied.

Rob picked up his ball from the hole and turned his attention, "Trae, when are you gonna get a girl?"

"Playa, I had two of them last night. I got what I need."

"Fool, please," Rob replied, "The girls at the strip club don't count." We all chuckled again as Trae waved off our joke.

My friend Trae was an older West Point grad. He got medically discharged as a Captain after an IED blew up his Humvee in Iraq. He broke his back and got pretty beat up, but he was relatively healthy now. After leaving the Army, he got his MBA from Harvard. At 45 years old, he was a Chief Financial Officer

155

for a startup that recently got acquired by a Fortune 500 company. In the 15 years I had known him, he never had a serious girlfriend.

We paused while he took his put. He missed by a few inches and finished it with a little tap.

"Look. I come down to Punta Cana once a quarter. I golf like this whenever I want and get treated like a king," he waved at the three caddies that had been following us and made a hand gesture for a beer.

"I ain't got to answer to nobody or get wifey's permission to come down here. I got a little Airbnb on the beach and I got twenty chicks I can call up if I want some pussy. And I'm stacking my paper. And it's all my money. I don't need to share it with no one. I don't need no wifey!"

We laughed at his exuberance for being a professional bachelor. We picked up our balls and gave our clubs to our caddies. In exchange, they handed us three ice cold Presidente beers.

"Let me ask you Rob," I said as we walked to the next hole, "I assume your wife makes a good amount of money owning her own law firm and what not. You and your wife are an *Alpha Couple*. How do you guys manage your finances? Do you use a joint account, or what?"

"Look man, it's simple. All our money goes into a joint account. We each get about a thousand dollars a month to spend on whatever we want. That's our individual fun money, but all the rest goes to that joint account. From there, we decide together if we want to set aside some for vacations, buy something nice for the kids, or whatever."

We surveyed the next hole.

"Par five. Looks like a dog leg left," Trae assessed.

"But doesn't she make a lot more money than you?" I asked Rob.

"Yeah, she does today, but that wasn't always the case. Heck, there were three months last year when she had a cash crunch and couldn't pay herself. Fortunately, the business is doing really good now. And when I get out of the Army, and Trae hires me as a VP, I'll be making more money than her!"

Trae pointed his beer bottle at Rob, "I told you to quit that Army bullshit and take your ass to Harvard."

"Quit the Army? Are you serious? Patton and Ike would be rolling in their graves if they heard you right now," we all laughed.

Rob returned his attention to me, "Everything goes to the joint account, then divide it up from there. It's not *your* money or *her* money. It's the *marriage's money*. Trust me, it's the best way."

Rob grabbed his club from the caddy and proceeded to tee off.

While I was at West Point, I joined Alpha Phi Alpha Fraternity, the nation's first intercollegiate historically African American fraternity. That support network of other Black cadets, officers, and professionals has been instrumental in my professional and personal life. Whenever we get together, we always have a great time talking about girls, finances, investing, and sharing stories about our time at West Point. Whether you are part of a cadet club, sports team, or just have a tight group of friends, I recommend you go out of your way to network with other old grads and continue to invest in those relationships over the years.

As a newly married man, I thought a lot about Rob's advice. Over time, I realized that most of the stress and financial frustration I had during my first marriage was because my ex-wife and I had different financial goals. Since we each kept most of our income separate, we were financially independent from each other. While it may be good for a single young professional to be financially independent, in a marriage, financial independence can be bad.

At the time of this writing, I've been married for about five years. During that time, I've met a lot of other dual professional couples, read a lot of books about marriage, did a lot of soul searching, and after action reviews about my first failed marriage. What I've learned is that a couple should set goals together and then work together to achieve those goals. Couples that are financially independent from each other are not incentivized to align their goals or work together financially.

Now, some people, especially women, think that they should be financially independent from their partner. They don't think that they should have to rely on their partner for anything. In a marriage, this can't be further from the truth.

Married couples should rely on each other for support, counsel, and for working together to achieve financial goals. Two together is stronger than two apart.

The caveat is that, although it's important for partners to be financially dependent on each other, it is equally important for them to share financial power and responsibilities. Many men find it difficult to share financial responsibility with their spouses, especially if they make more money. Our society's traditional idea of patriarch marriages usually has the man of the house bringing home the bacon and controlling the finances. This is a damaging paradigm for marriages, especially for dual professional couples.

In a marriage, one partner should never have more power over finances than the other. The power to manage a household's finances is not proportional to how much money each partner makes. Each partner should have equal power to manage how the couple's money is spent and invested regardless of how much they contribute to the budget.

Eventually, my new wife and I adopted the financial management strategy recommended by my friend. We first made a joint budget and then decided how much we would save in our TSP and 401K. Over time, we were able to max out our TSP and 401K ($19,500 each), maxed out our Roth IRAs ($6,000 each), and then deposited all our take home income into a single joint account.

Usually, we each get about $1,000 per month to spend on whatever we want. The rest stays in the joint account until we divvy it up between expenses, savings, investments, or travel funds. We do not have a financial advisor, instead we prefer to manage our investments ourselves. We meet with our CPA once per quarter to go over our taxes. Twice a year we have a calendaring and financial planning weekend, were we book a hotel room at the local Ritz Carlton and then spend the weekend planning out our financial goals and calendar for the upcoming year.

My wife and I are both busy professionals. Between her job, my career, and my side hustles, we each work 60 to 80 hours per week. We thoroughly enjoy the work that we do. About half the time, my wife works from home, and I'm fortunate to be in a job where I am home almost every day by 6:00 pm. We have plenty of time to spend with each other and with our daughter, but not a lot of time for tasks like cleaning toilets. Therefore, our joint expenses include a weekly housecleaner, landscaper, and nanny who does our grocery shopping and light cooking.

Depositing all of our income in a joint account and treating all of our income as joint instead of mine and hers, has helped us simplify our lives. This strategy has also been an incredibly powerful force to help us work together towards our financial goals. Whether you are a millionaire or lieutenant, if you are married to someone that you love and want to spend the rest of your life with them, then I recommend you direct deposit all income into a joint account, treat all income as the marriage's, have open and honest discussions about money, and set financial goals as a couple.

Some people have concerns that this strategy may put them at financial risk in the event of a divorce. They worry that if they make a lot more money than their spouse, that their spouse can more easily take half of their savings in a divorce. I know this to be true because I experienced it and had similar concerns before marrying my current wife.

The truth is that for the most part, in a divorce, a wife is entitled to half of all assets earned during the marriage. So even if a high-earning husband saved $1 million during his marriage to a stay-at-home wife, that stay-at-home wife would be entitled to $500,000 even though she never worked. In a marriage, any savings or interest earned during the marriage is marital property and equally divisible regardless of who earned it. This is the case even if you have a prenuptial agreement, which usually only covers pre-marital property.

I know that I am very fortunate to be married to another professional who makes a six-figure salary. It can be very difficult for dependent spouses to find jobs and develop a professional career when the military moves us every two to three years. I also know that many military spouses prefer to be home makers. Being a home maker is equally as respectable as being a working professional.

Caring for a home and children is difficult and it can be expensive if you hire help. A house cleaner cost about $5,000 a year. Full time daycare for two children can cost about $20,000 per year. If a dependent spouse only makes $35,000 per year ($17.50 per hour), then the cost-benefit of a full-time job is usually not worth it. It can seem pointless to work 40 hours a week to make $35,000 when childcare expenses are $25,000. Taking home an extra $10,000 per year is not nearly worth the cost of missing out on hours upon hours of key developmental time in your child's life. This is one reason why many spouses choose to be home caretakers instead of working. The decision for a spouse to be a home caretaker is incredibly admirable and especially understandable given the military lifestyle.

It is difficult to build wealth as a single income family, but it certainly is not impossible. All of the investment principles I've learned throughout my life equally apply to dual-income and single-income families. It may take a single-income family a little longer to achieve millionaire status, but I know many families that were still able to surpass the milestone.

When it comes to building wealth, the most important decision I ever made was attending West Point. The formal and informal education, the network, and the military career associated with it have had a tremendous impact on my personal finances and life in ways that are difficult to quantify. I know that I would not be a millionaire today if not for that decision.

The second most important financial decision I ever made was in choosing who to marry. When I married my first wife, I chose poorly. Fortunately, I got it right the second time around. It certainly helps financially that my wife is a working professional and that we are a dual income family. Regardless of her income, it is more important that we have aligned our professional, personal, and financial goals. We communicate regularly about finances and we merged our financial lives just like we merged our personal lives. Financial union is a pillar of building a powerful marriage.

LET'S RECAP

Who you marry is one of the most significant decisions that will impact your net worth and lifetime earnings.

Married couples must work together to achieve shared financial goals. This requires shared responsibility of finances and open and honest conversations about money.

Whether a dual-income or single-income family, the best joint financial strategy is to direct deposit both partners' income into a joint account and then work together to divvy up the income.

In a marriage, all income and earnings are joint income and earnings, regardless of who works or earns more money.

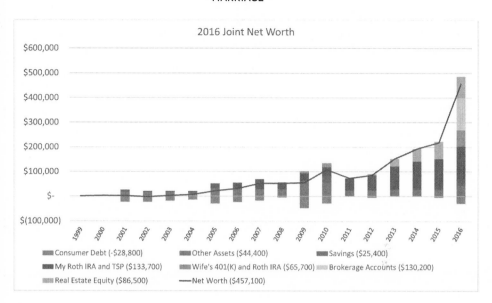

2016 Joint Net Worth

Legend:
- Consumer Debt (-$28,800)
- Other Assets ($44,400)
- Savings ($25,400)
- My Roth IRA and TSP ($133,700)
- Wife's 401(K) and Roth IRA ($65,700)
- Brokerage Accounts ($130,200)
- Real Estate Equity ($86,500)
- Net Worth ($457,100)

SIDE HUSTLES

People are surprised whenever they find out that I own a coffee roaster business. No, I'm not famous like Black Rifle Coffee, but I admit that they inspired me. It's just a small hobby of mine that turned into a business.

I started roasting coffee after my wife and I visited Kona on our Hawaiian honeymoon. We were really impressed with the quality and deliciousness of the Hawaiian coffee and thought that the local coffee shop down the street from us in Kansas City should also carry Kona coffee. We began to explore ways that we could import coffee from Hawaii to the mainland and stumbled into roasting.

Shortly after returning from Hawaii, I converted our garage to a roasting business. Today, I buy the beans, roast them, package them, and then sell the coffee beans and coffee on evenings and weekends. I bought a used mini-RV trailer and converted it into a coffee and snacks stand. On the weekends, I take the stand to local farmers markets, little league games, and festivals where I sell my coffee and snacks.

I usually take the coffee stand out on Friday nights, Saturdays, and Sundays. I also have a high school kid that helps me out. I had to hire the kid because there are many weekends when I'm out of town and the business must go on regardless of if I'm there or not. My wife also joins me from time to time to keep me company.

It cost me about $14,000 to get the business started. My initial investments included the roasting equipment, packaging, marketing material, other supplies, and the mini-RV. After I pay my employee, who is a 1099 independent contractor, I am lucky to make about $300 per month. The business isn't going to make me a multi-millionaire, at least not at the current rate. It's just something that I enjoy doing and that I hope will eventually become more profitable.

In addition to my coffee roaster business, I also own a real estate business (for my rental properties), a new publishing business (for this book), and my wife owns a coaching business. Some of these businesses have been more profitable than others, but all have been extremely rewarding. Additionally, as business owners, we take full advantage of business tax deductions which save us tens of thousands of dollars each year.

Owning a business is not for everyone, but I've found that many officers, at one point or another, consider starting a business on the side (technically, even owning and managing rental properties can count as a business). A side hustle can be a fun and rewarding experience and a good source of additional income.

If I could share one lesson to aspiring business owners, it would be that If you sell a good or service, or have plans to sell a good or service, you can start your own business today. As a business owner, you can take advantage of tax deductions which can save you money and allow you to invest more back into the business. Generally speaking, to start a business, all you need is a product or service and a plan to become profitable. You don't need an LLC to start a business, nor do you need to be currently profitable.

Here is an example of how I started with my little coffee roaster business. My business started the moment that I told myself, "I'm going to start roasting my own Hawaiian coffee and plan to sell it."

From that moment on, well before I sold my first cup of joe, I began documenting all of my business-related expenses. I spent about $7,000 on the mini-RV and subsequent conversion to a coffee stand, $5,000 on the roaster and packaging equipment, $1,000 on coffee beans (we have a lot of beans!), and another $1,000 on marketing material and other administrative costs. I repurposed my garage and home office for the business, which would have cost me at least $1,000 per month if I wanted to rent a similar space in the city. In summary, the $12,000 worth of workshop and office space, plus the $14,000 in capital expenses, added up to about $26,000 in tax-deductible expenses the first year of my business, most of which was before I had an LLC and before I was profitable.

My wife and I are in the 25% tax bracket, which means that deducting an additional $26,000 from our taxes saved us about $6,500 that first year. Year after year, the tax deductions from our businesses continue to save us a few thousand dollars per year in taxes.

Now that the business has been going for a few years, we have a regular income and I pay taxes on that. After paying for supplies and for my contractor, my take home pay is about $300 each month. After taxes, it comes out to about $225 per month. It's not a lot, but it's certainly something. I estimate that at my current rate it will take me about 5 years to break even on my initial investment.

I have an LLC now for my coffee business and my monthly cash flow is profitable, but that was not always the case. For the first few months I was selling my beans at farmer's markets and I didn't have an LLC. My county did not require an LLC to sell at farmers markets, so I didn't get one. I operated perfectly legally as an unregistered sole proprietorship. Eventually, I registered my business as an LLC, but not at first.

Generally, the IRS treats *sole proprietor business owners* and *independent contractors* the same as *self-employed*. And for tax purposes, being a registered company is not necessarily required (although it may help in the slim chance that you ever get audited). There are some caveats to when you may need an LLC, which I'll mention later, but first let's define what it means to be an LLC.

An Limited Liability Company is a registered business structure where the owner(s) is generally not personally liable for the company's debts or liabilities. In other words, if a customer sued you, a properly structured LLC may help limit your personal liability (although not guaranteed). The claimant would be able to go after your business assets and financial accounts, but would have a difficult time going after your personal assets or money. An LLC provides business owners with some financial protections, but the LLC title has little to do with the underlying business activities.

While an LLC is an example of a *registered* business, it is perfectly legal in many cases to operate an *unregistered* business if you follow local, state, and federal laws. There are some cases, where you need to register a business before you can practice, for example if you are a doctor, lawyer, or engineer, but for many businesses, such as photographers, artists, or YouTubers, an LLC is not required.

Although most home businesses don't need to register an LLC, registering an LLC is actually quite easy. For most states, you can register an LLC in a few minutes online for $100-$200 per year.

Every state has their own LLC regulations, and you should probably check all pertinent laws before doing business in your state. There are also different types of registered businesses such as partnerships, C Corps, and S Corps. Sole proprietorships are the most common structure for unregistered businesses, and LLCs are the most common for registered businesses. You should do some research to make sure that you pick a business structure that fits your business needs.

For sole proprietorship, LLCs, and any business for that matter, the key is that you keep track of expenses and income, and report your net income and losses on your tax returns. As soon as you decide to start a business with a profit motive, you should start recording your expenses. Your business expenses may be tax deductible long before you have a paying customer. This is another important point — you don't need to be profitable to own a business or claim tax deductions. The IRS website says, "You do not need to actually make a profit to be in a trade or business as long as you have a profit motive. You do need, however, to make ongoing efforts to further the interests of your business."

If you need an example of a non-profitable business, just look at Tesla. Tesla was unprofitable for over eight years! They lost hundreds of millions of dollars year after year before finally making a profit. Similar principles and laws apply to your home-based businesses.

Furthermore, you can operate a business from your home, on a part-time basis while serving in the military, and still take advantage of business tax benefits. The IRS website says, "You do not have to carry on regular full-time business activities to be self-employed. Having a part-time business in addition to your regular job or business also may be self-employment."

When it comes to businesses, the key aspect to understand, and the reason why I wrote this chapter, is because U.S. tax regulations favor business owners!

Small business owners power America's economy and for decades Congress has enacted favorable tax laws to encourage small business investments. Just because you are in the military or have a full-time job, does not mean that you cannot also have a business on the side, if that is something you desire.

You should do your own research or consult with a Certified Public Accountant before making important tax decisions, but here are some general examples of potential tax-deductible expenses.

- The expense of your home office, studio, or workshop
- Office expenses like a portion of your internet, phone bill, or supplies
- Cost of advertising like websites, business cards, and logos
- Car or vehicle expenses if necessary for your business
- Education required for your profession
- Insurance, certain taxes, and fees

If you have profit motives, and keep good documentation, you can deduct many of these expenses. Reducing your taxable income through qualified business tax deductions can save you thousands of dollars each year in taxes!

Now, an important question that business owners should evaluate is whether it is better to itemize tax deductions or to take a standard deduction.

For the 2020 tax year, the standard tax deduction for singles is about $12,400. Meaning that if you make $60,000 a year, the IRS will tax you on $47,600. The deductible reduces your tax burden.

If your business income is minimal and all your tax deductions for the year (including personal deductions like mortgage interest, qualified donations, education expenses, etc.) are less than a few thousand dollars, then it is probably easier to take the standard deduction. However, if your business expenses and other deductions exceed the standard deduction, then it is probably better to itemize your expenses.

Whether you itemize deductions or not, maintaining good business income and expense records is always a good practice. To itemize your business expenses, most small business owners will use an IRS Schedule C to report income or loss from a business operated as a sole proprietor.

Although the amount of information required can seem intimidating at first, don't let that deter you. Online programs like TurboTax will walk you through many of these documents and, if you can afford it, hiring a CPA is a great investment once your business gets up and running.

Even if starting a business isn't for you, understanding tax codes is an extremely important aspect of building long term wealth.

As your business grows, you may want to eventually register an LLC, set up business bank accounts, get business insurance, get a federal EIN, hire a CPA, and hire attorneys to help you. But when you are just starting your business, the key is to focus on the most important aspects that will help your business grow. Usually, the most important thing a new business owner can do is: 1) focus on delivering a great product or service to their customers and 2) keep good income and expense records.

I should also point out that according to various Department of Defense regulations and policies, service members may be denied from participating in outside employment or owning a business if it interferes with official duties, if it will detract from readiness, pose a security risk, mis-represent the government, create a conflict of interest, or create the appearance of a conflict of interest with his or her official duties. This is why service members should get approval from their chain of command before starting a business.

This even includes activities like driving for Lyft or Uber. When I asked my commander if I could start my coffee business he gladly approved and was more curious than anything else. If you live in on-post housing or plan to do business on a base, check with your installation for local policies concerning on post business.

As an Army officer, your duty to the nation and official responsibilities should always come first, but unless you are on a deployment, the Army doesn't expect you to work 24 hours a day seven days a week. Most of us have extra free time to devote to a business, whether it is managing rental properties, driving for Uber, selling art on Etsy, making instructional videos on YouTube, crypto-mining, or owning a food truck. The list is endless.

As an added benefit, if you start a side hustle while in the military it can help give you career options when you decide to retire. For example, former Green Beret Evan Hafer founded his Black Rifle Coffee Company while he was still serving in Special Forces. When I retire, I don't think I want to take my coffee roaster business to that level, but maybe I will become a full-time author or business consultant instead.

If you have a business idea, go for it! Side hustles can be personally and financially rewarding.

LET'S RECAP

Service members should get chain of command approval before working outside of normal military duties.

You can start a business and claim business tax deductions if you sell goods or services, or plan to sell goods or services, in good faith to make a profit.

A key component of any business is to keep meticulous records of your income and expenses. There are also many commonly overlooked tax deductions to owning a home business, such as the cost of a home office.

Check all pertinent laws and policies before doing business in your state, county, or on base. Additionally, check IRS regulations or consult with a lawyer or tax professional if required.

A side hustle can be a fun and financially rewarding experience.

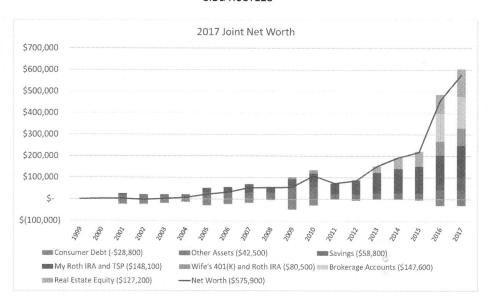

ADVANCE TRADING

After a short two years at Fort Leavenworth, I got reassigned to Headquarters Department of the Army (HQDA) staff in the Pentagon. I tried avoiding the Pentagon for years, but ultimately it was like a black hole whose gravity I could not escape.

Pentagon assignments are good and bad. They are bad because most of your energy in the Pentagon is spent navigating bureaucracy. At times, it seems like the smallest decision requires dozens of inefficient Councils of Colonels followed by even more bureaucratic General Officer Steering Committees. There is meeting after mind-numbing meeting where presenters drone on. I swear that my eyesight deteriorated a full point from trying to constantly read size 10 font PowerPoint charts—I hate PowerPoint.

Despite the negatives, the Pentagon is an incredible place to work. During my time there, I realized that the bureaucracy exists for a reason, namely to protect tax payers, ensure that investments support the Commander-in-Chief's priorities, and to enact the budget, appropriations, and laws dictated by Congress. The bureaucracy may be inefficient, but in many ways that is by design. Working in the Pentagon made me more appreciative of our nation's complicated three-party system and the checks and balances that exist between the executive and legislative branches.

One of the more interesting aspect that I observed is that most of the big decisions were not made in largely attended General Officer Steering Committees. Instead, most of the big decisions were made by a Bunch of Guys or Gals Sitting Around a Table (BOGSAT). These small, informal meetings between senior decision makers had huge impacts to program investments and strategic operations.

On one occasion, I got tasked to attend a meeting between a lieutenant general and congressional staffer from the Senate Appropriations Committee.

It was a meeting that opened my eyes to how decisions are made at the highest levels of our government.

The general and I met the staffer in his office at the Capitol Building. Our agenda was to talk about a software project that our office had been developing in addition to another program, which I'll call Program X (not actual name).

The general greeted the staffer, "Hey Bob, good to see you again."

"You too Bob."

Yes, they were both named Bob.

The general got to it, "Look Bob, I know your schedule is tight, so I want to jump right in. I want to chat with you about Program X but first the good lieutenant colonel here is going to show you the logistics management system that our team has been working on."

The only reason I was in the meeting was because I had been helping a group of soldiers to develop a supply chain management system and I knew the application better than most people in the headquarters. Normally the Army doesn't trust general officers with operating computers. So, it was my job to demo the software which I rehearsed meticulously with a handful of colonels several times leading up to this meeting.

Normally, I wouldn't get invited to a close door meeting between a three-star and a very influential staffer. In public, these staffers command the same respect as four-star generals. Staffer Bob was impressed with the demo. "Wow. That is amazing. This is going to save our taxpayers a lot of money."

"I know!" said General Bob.

After they talked about the software a little more, General Bob continued, "While we have some time, I wanted to talk to you about Program X."

"Of course," Bob said, "What's on your mind?"

Over the next 15 minutes, LTG Bob discussed why the program was a priority and Staffer Bob discussed his concerns about funding the program.

At the end of the meeting, Staffer Bob commented, "I think Program X is in a good place."

"Thanks Bob," the LTG said, "It's good to see you again."

"You too Bob."

Over the next few days, LTG Bob and I had more meetings with different staffers. Additionally, Program X was discussed in various program reviews, councils of colonels, and general officer steering committees, but despite the PowerPoints and bureaucratic churn, I got the strong impression that the really important decisions were made when a bunch of guys named Bob just sat around a table and talked.

The concerted information campaign and road show around Capitol Hill worked. A few weeks later, the appropriations committees published their budget. Program X was fully funded $500 million.

The Pentagon is an incredibly complex ecosystem. It's a huge bureaucracy, there are layers and layers of red tape to get anything done, and most people, including myself, spend their entire days attending one meeting after another after another. As a LTC, I am frequently one of the lowest ranking officers in meetings and I usually sit quietly in the back of the room taking notes.

Despite the bureaucracy, and occasional feeling of being a Plebe, the Pentagon and National Capital Region is a marvel. When I served at HQDA, I was front row to watch how the sausage was made. Terms like the Senate Armed Service Committees, the Presidential Budget, and National Defense Strategy took on new meaning. I learned how the President's defense priorities flowed down through the Armed Services and how different congressional staff members, combatant commanders, program executive offices, and defense contractors could affect the national budget. More importantly, I got to see how the decisions we made affected soldiers across the force. I saw first-hand how our actions shaped the future of our Army with new weapon systems, technology development, and program funding.

When I was a young captain, I accepted and inventoried whatever equipment I was issued without really knowing why the Army decided that I should have it. Later, as an operations officer, I began to see how my squadron's missions fit into the larger division strategy. And now as a lieutenant colonel, I understand the higher-level inputs, outputs, and gears that drive national defense.

In many ways, my growth as an Army officer paralleled my growth as an investor. When I was a lieutenant, I invested in companies I liked without really questioning them. Now, as a more seasoned investor I have a greater understanding of company operations, financial metrics, and the broader markets. Similar to how there are many stakeholders involved in government financial decisions, I've also learned to appreciate the roles of different stake holders in the stock markets. In a publicly traded company, the C-suite executives, institutional investors, retail investors, customers, and even the government all play an important role in determining the stock price. Frequently a few guys or gals, making decisions while sitting around a table, can have huge impacts to your investment portfolio, especially if you begin using some of the trading strategies that I discuss in this chapter.

I've found that most professionals who are serious about building wealth, eventually become interested in trading stocks. After a few successful stock picks, most investors naturally become interested in more advanced stock trading strategies like trading options or using technical analysis. This chapter is about some of those more advanced trading strategies.

I couldn't possibly cover all of the advanced trading strategies, but I'll cover a few of the big ones and share my thoughts on each. Advanced trading strategies are incredibly complex, and I don't claim to be an expert in any of them. I'm merely sharing my simple understanding of them along with some lessons that I've learned.

To begin, all of these strategies are based upon the stock market. For the most part, these strategies are alternative ways of trading stocks, other than the traditional buy and hold method. Most of these strategies have greater volatility than normal stock trading. If the market or underlying asset is doing well, these strategies can return exponential gains. Inversely, if the market or asset performs poorly, your investment can exponentially decrease in value or even become nearly worthless almost overnight. With advance strategies, the risk is greater and margin for error is smaller.

These strategies offer greater rewards and greater risks. As such, they are more susceptible to swings in the market. Unpredictable events like earnings call misses, company mergers, new issuance of convertible notes, or the CEO's Tweets can quickly drive the value of an investment up or down. It is difficult to predict these events, but the results can have huge impacts on your investments. If you are overexposed on a position when they occur, the results could be incredibly detrimental to your investment. This is a particular risk for the strategies in this chapter.

Strategy 1: Swing Trading

In my previous chapter on stocks, I talked about how I approach deep value trading. The same principles apply to my more advanced trading. I trade in companies whose mission I believe in, I try to avoid trading emotionally, and I conduct due diligence and learn about companies before I make an investment. I constantly assess my risk and rewards and I stick to the sectors that I am bullish in like automation, semiconductors, genomics, and artificial intelligence.

My basic deep value strategy is to buy and hold stocks for a few years at a time. I make a decision and then let the results of that decision play out for a year or more. In contrast, a more advanced strategy is shorter term swing trading. Instead of buying and holding for a year or more, I sometimes trade stocks that I hold for only a few days or weeks.

The key to swing trading is recognizing short term trends and naturally occurring oscillations in the stock market.

As an example, during the Coronavirus pandemic I bought and sold short term positions in pandemic stocks like Peloton (PTON) and Zoom (ZM). My short-term investments during the pandemic gave me a nice 150% profit.

Generally speaking, I avoid cash in my accounts. Usually, I have no more than 1% to 5% cash in my brokerage account if any at all. Instead, I prefer to move investments in between high-risk and low-risk stocks during market volatility.

As an example, if I think the market is in a bear pattern, I'll decrease my position in risky tech stocks like Lemonade Insurance (LMND) or Schrödinger (SDGR) and increase my position in more stable large cap companies like Apple (AAPL) and Amazon (AMZN). When the market is doing poorly, my more volatile tech stocks can decrease 10% to 15% in a day while my large cap stocks may only decrease 2% to 5%. Inversely, if the market is red and I expect a positive correction, I'll load up on the more volatile stocks.

Swing trading can be emotionally challenging. When an investment is up 25% and the entire market is green, it is easy to feel optimistic that the market will continue to go up. Frequently, these green days are the time when you should sell your swing trades. Conversely, on negative days, when the stock market looks like a blood bath, it can be emotionally difficult to invest more money when your losses for the day exceed tens of thousands of dollars. Yet, these red days are frequently the time when swing traders need to be the most bullish. To be an effective swing trader, you frequently need to invest against your own emotions.

When swing trading, it is also difficult to time the peaks and troughs of the market. Ideally, you want to sell when the stock is high and buy when the stock is low, but it is easier said than done. I have personally screwed up my timing many times and lost thousands of dollars as a result. I've also timed it right on a few occasions which have been extremely profitable.

In 2020 for example, the Coronavirus pandemic hit the world. From February to March, I saw my portfolio value drop by 25%. Generally, I avoid cash in my brokerage account, but in March 2020, I made an exception.

On March 13th, the market looked like it was going to recover. President Trump was optimistic, and the market rose about 6% in one day. While things were looking good, I sold all of my stocks and mutual funds and moved completely to cash in my brokerage accounts, approximately $150,000. Over the next week, the market continued to decline another 25%.

A week later, I began to reinvest in the market. During this time, New York was in lock down, and the pandemic looked like it was going to destroy the economy. People acknowledged that we were in a recession and expected the market to continue to decline even worse than the Great Depression. During these bleak times, I began reinvesting in the market. Not only did I reinvest the cash in my account, but my wife and I also scraped together another $50,000 and added it to our brokerage account. Swing trading during the 2020 recession and subsequent recovery helped us return a 100% profit in less than 9 months.

Buying and then selling stock less than a year and one day later, results in short term gains tax. Which is taxed as part of your normal income. While stocks held for longer than that are taxed at the lower capital gains tax rate. My average swing trade is for a month or less (sometimes only a few hours), which would not qualify for capital gains. This is one reason why I sometimes swing trade in my Roth IRA. It's risky to use these trading strategies in a Roth IRA, because if you lose money in there, you are limited in how much you can replace. However, a Roth IRA can provide exceptional tax benefits.

Strategy 2: Leverage

If you trade with leverage, it means that you borrow money to buy stock. When you buy a house, you are using leverage. For example, if you make a $40,000 down payment to buys a $200,000 house, you are actually using your $40,000 to leverage a $200,000 purchase. That would be a 5x leverage which in stock trading, would be also be called a 20% margin. You need to fund 20% of the investment yourself and the rest you can fund with borrowed money.

Most brokerages will approve a 50% margin for a basic retail investor. If you had an account with a 50% margin, you could purchase twice as much stock as you would be able to without margin.

Let's say for example, that you have $5,000 in your non-margin brokerage account and Apple trades at $100 per share. Normally, you could buy 50 shares of AAPL with your $5,000. If the stock price increases 10% to $110 per share, you could then sell your 50 shares for a net profit of $500.

If instead, you bought AAPL stock with a 50% margin, you could buy $10,000 worth of AAPL, or 100 shares, with an initial deposit of $5,000. If the stock price increases to $110 per share, you could then sell your 100 shares for a net profit of $1,000. In this case, a 2x leverage doubled your return. Instead of profiting $500, you profited $1,000. A 10% increase in AAPL resulted a 20% profit.

A 50% margin can double your potential returns. Similarly, a 25% margin, or 4x leverage, would quadruple your returns. If you are confident that a stock will go up, then leverage is a great way to increase your return on investment greater than the growth of underlying asset.

On the flip side though, if the stock goes down, you can also lose money much quicker. In our scenario, if you bought AAPL with a 50% margin and AAPL stock decreased to $90, then instead of losing $500, you would lose $1,000.

If you elect to use a margin account, your account will have a minimum margin and each individual stock will also have its own minimum margin maintenance requirements. For example, the minimum maintenance requirement for AAPL may be 35%. If the initial value of your equity in the stock decreases less than 35% of the initial purchase price, your brokerage can issue a maintenance call and automatically sell your stock for you at a loss.

In our example, if the stock price of AAPL dropped from $100 to $70, then your 100 shares of AAPL would be worth $7,000. Since you bought half the stocks with borrowed money, your equity would be worth $3,500, which is 35% of the initial investment of $10,000. In this case, your brokerage would issue a maintenance or margin call requesting you to deposit more funds into your account. If you failed to deposit more funds, then the brokerage could sell your assets for you.

These margin calls can happen fast. Sometimes you may have a day or two to deposit funds, but in other instances they can demand immediate deposits. Failure to comply can result in your stocks getting liquidated, often sold to the lowest bidder. In this case, the brokerage would sell your shares of AAPL at $70 per share, which would be a 60% loss for you.

In a previous chapter, I said that the fastest way to build wealth is to have a concentrated portfolio. That statement was partially correct. The full statement is:

The fastest way to build wealth is to have a concentrated portfolio with leverage. This is also the fastest way to lose wealth.

Margin calls are bad. Historically, it seems like they happen at the most inopportune times. For example, during a momentary dip in a stock price immediately before the stock rallies to all-time highs. Many investors have lost massive amounts of money due to margin calls.

An example of this occurred during the January 2021 GameStop rally. During the rally, GME became extremely volatile, sometimes swinging 50% down or 100% up or down day-to-day. During the rally, some brokerage services changed the margin requirement on GME from 50% to 100%. Anyone who purchased GME with margin was immediately forced to sell their positions. This occurred even as GME was rallying to its 52-week all-time high. It is understandable why so many retail investors were pissed off that they got forced out of their position as the stock price was increasing.

You can't use margin in an IRA account, so this strategy only applies to trading in a regular brokerage account. In my brokerage account, my margin limit is 50%. I usually keep my balance at 70% or higher to avoid maintenance calls.

Margin has its risks, but overall using leverage is a method to increase your rates of return faster than the change in the underlying asset. This is true whether the stock price goes up and down.

Strategy 3: Options

Option trading is perhaps the most complex advanced trading strategy and the most difficult to fully understand. Some option strategies are not much different than buying stocks while other options strategies are more similar to playing the lottery. There are option strategies that can appeal to almost any risk tolerance level.

There are so many different types of option strategies that it would require a separate book to explain all of them. I won't explain all of them, because I generally only use one option type. It's the simplest to understand—*the call option.*

Options are contracts between a buyer and a seller. In its simplest form a call option is a contract that gives the buyer the right to buy 100 shares of stock at a later date at a set price. The key elements of a call option are the expiration date and the strike price.

Let's say for example, it is January 2021 and Apple stock is trading at $100 per share. You want to buy a call option for AAPL that has an expiration date of 1/23/2022 and a strike price is $120. This option bid price is $19 and the ask price is $21. Which means that another buyer is willing to pay $19 for this contract and a seller is willing to sell the contract for $21.

The asking price is the price per share. You place a bid for $20 and the seller sells you the contract. Since the standard option contract is for 100 shares, the actual call option costs you $2,000 plus a minor fee of $0.65. As long as you own that option, you have an open contract with the seller who may be another retail investor or firm.

The call option gives you the right to buy 100 shares of Apple stock at the strike price of $120 any time before January 23rd, 2022. If you wanted to execute that contract, you could deposit $12,000 into your account and call your brokerage to request to execute it. The seller of the contract would then be on the hook to sell you 100 shares of AAPL at $120 each. With $12,000 you would buy 100 shares of AAPL from the contract seller. If the seller had 100 shares of AAPL in her brokerage account, she would sell you those stocks (this is called a *covered call*), otherwise the seller would need to buy 100 shares of AAPL at the market price and then sell you those (that would be a *naked call*).

As the buyer of the call option, you would not know if the seller sold you a covered or naked call, and it wouldn't make a difference to you as a buyer. Either way, you'd get your 100 shares of AAPL for $120 each. The $2,000 you spent to buy that contract would be lost. Therefore, the net cost to buy 100 shares of AAPL using the contract would be $14,000 plus fees ($2,000 to open the call contract and $12,000 to execute it).

If the stock is trading at $100 per share, you would never execute the contract because it would be cheaper to buy 100 shares of AAPL stock on the open exchange instead of spending $120 per share through your contract.

If in December 2021, a month before the contract's expiration date, the stock price of AAPL shot up from $100 per share to $170 per share, then it would be profitable to execute the contract. At $170 per share, 100 shares of AAPL would cost $17,000. Since your call contract gives you the ability to buy 100 shares of AAPL at $120 each, you could save a significant amount of money by executing your contract. The cost of executing the contract would be $12,000 plus fees, which is less than the cost of buying 100 shares of AAPL stock at $17,000.

You could execute the call option for $12,000 which would make you the owner of 100 shares of AAPL. You could then immediately sell those shares for $170 each, or $17,000 total. Your gain would be $5,000. Accounting for your initial $2,000 investment to buy the call contract, your net profit would be $3,000 minus any fees. In this scenario, AAPL stock price increased from $100 to $170 (70% gain) and the value of your call option increased from $2,000 to $5,000 (150% gain).

In practice you would not actually need to call the brokerage to execute the contract. Instead, you would buy the option (open the contract) for $2,000 and then sell (close the contract) for $5,000. The process of buying and selling options is not that much more difficult than buying and selling stocks.

Inversely, if instead of rising to $170, AAPL never rose above $120 before the expiration day, then the value of your contract will gradually approach $0. If you do not execute your contract or sell to close before the expiration date, the option contract simply expires. Your $2,000 initial investment would disappear (profit for the seller).

In essence, a call option is a bet that the stock price will increase before the expiration date, and hopefully increase to a level where it would be profitable to execute or sell (close) your contract. Similar to using margin, a basic call option strategy can increase your profits at a greater percentage than the increase in value of the underlying asset. Dissimilar to margin, options have expiration dates. Option contracts are only valid for a certain period of time which presents another type of risk.

If all this talk about options and calls made your head spin, then you are not alone. Option trading is extremely complicated, and I only explained the simplest form of option trading. There are countless other strategies such as: puts, covered calls, bull call spreads, bear call puts, married puts, long straddles, long call butterfly spreads, and many more.

Option trading is one of the most complex investment strategies. They can be extremely high risk and remarkably high reward. Option trading is riskier than simply buying common stock, but the higher risk can result in higher returns if your strategy is successful.

Depending on your time horizon and strike price, you can pick options that are low or high risk. I've had options that have increased 140% and then decreased to negative 50% on the same day!

By selecting different expiration dates and selecting different strike prices, savvy investors can select call options that meet their personal risk tolerance preference.

For investors that are new to options, I first recommend that they become familiar with basic stock trading. If an investor has never traded stocks, they should not jump into option trading.

To begin with options, I recommend a similar approach as I recommended earlier with stock trading. Pick companies that you like, spend a few weeks conducting research and due diligence, and spend a few weeks following the option chains before you buy an option. You can even pretend to buy an option and then follow its price using a virtual portfolio like those available on Yahoo Finance.

To buy options on most brokerage services, you first apply to trade options in your account. Once approved, you go to the option trading page. From there you search for the stock symbol and then select the expiration date. For first time option traders, I recommend an expiration date that is at least three to six months in the future.

After you select the expiration date, you will see the option chain for that date. The option chain includes all of the available strike prices. For first time option traders, I generally prefer in-the-money (ITM) calls. An ITM call is an option whose strike price is less than the current stock price. A lower risk first-time strategy is to buy an ITM call that is about 10% to 20% less than the current stock price. Here is an example of an option chain for PTON for two different expiration dates. These approximate prices are from February 10th, 2021. At the time of this chart, PTON was trading at about $145 per share.

Peloton (PTON) Option Chains
Today's Date: February 12, 2021

February 19, 2021 (1 week in the future)		September 17, 2021 (7 months in the future)	
Strike Price	Last Price	Strike Price	Last Price
$100	$44.50	$100	$56.50
$115	$40.00	$115	$49.00
$130	$15.50	$130	$36.50
$145	$2.80	$145	$31.00
$160	$0.19	$160	$24.00
$185	$0.02	$185	$18.65
$200	$0.01	$200	$14.70

You notice that the February 19th, $200 call is trading cheap, a mere penny per share. This near-term out-the-money call is cheap because it is the highest risk. It is extremely unlikely that PTON will increase from $145 to $200 in less than 7 days. But if, by some miracle, PTON increased to $250, imagine how much profit you would be able to make if you bought an option for $1 (100 x $0.01) and could then sell it for $5,000 (100 x $50). Although extremely unlikely, the ROI would be 5,000%.

Meanwhile, the February 19th, $100 strike is more expensive because PTON will likely continue to trade around $145 for the next week. You will notice that for these weekly options, the in-the-money prices plus the strike price track closely with the value of the stock. The $115 strike price plus the $40 last price is only slightly more expensive than value as the stock, which is $145. These in-the-money options change prices proportionally to the underlying asset. Of the available options, they have lower risk, but still more risk than the underlying stock. Also, remember that standard option contracts are for 100 shares of stock, so you need to multiply these list prices by 100. The $115 strike price contract actually trades for $4,000.

The further out, September 17th options cost more because they have more intrinsic value. A certain level of optimism is priced into each of the contracts based upon supply and demand of available options. These further out options give the stock price more time to fluctuate, and also give the option holder more time to select the best time to sell. They have lower temporal risk.

An option holder can sell to close their call option any time before the expiration date. It's not uncommon for me to close an option three months or more before an expiration date if I think the stock price has plateaued. Sometimes it is better to lock in profits or losses instead of stressing closer to the expiration date.

As a real-world example, I'm writing this in February 2021. Peloton is currently trading at $145. At the moment, I'm bullish on Peloton so I bought a call option for September 17th, 2021, at a strike price of $130, for a cost of $36.50 per share, or $3,650 total. In shorthand, this contract would be abbreviated as "Sep 17 '21 $130 C." Since I paid $36.50 per share for this call, my breakeven point for PTON is $166.50. To definitively make a profit before September 17th, I need the stock price to exceed $166.50.

If you are reading this in the future, you can look up the PTON stock chart to see how well I did.

Between now and September, I will continuously assess the performance of Peloton. There are a variety of factors that would lead me to sell to close my option contract. For example, if Peloton starts declining or if I became bearish on Peloton, I may sell to limit my loss. If the stock price dropped from $145 to below the strike price of $130 per share, the value of my call option would decrease dramatically. Conversely, if Peloton does really well and rallies above $200 per share in March, I may sell to close in order to lock in my profits. Once a call option becomes deep in the money like this, it loses a lot of its intrinsic value and begins to track closely with the stock price. A rally above $200 would likely increase the value of my call to $80 or more, which would be a 2x ROI in less than two months. If I was still bullish on Peloton, at that point, I may sell my deep in the money call option and roll it to another call option that was closer to the strike price and maybe at a later expiration date.

Generally, deep in the money call options are less risky than call options at the money. Inversely, out of the money calls get riskier. The further out the money the strike price, the riskier it becomes. Calls that are far out the money, and especially ones that expire the current week, are frequently called weekly lottos because the odds of getting a profit are about the same as playing a lotto ticket. The payoff can be just as big too.

Far out the money calls can sometimes trade for a few dollars. For example, one Reddit trader named *WSBgod* reported that they bought Tesla calls at a

$1,000 strike price for $3 per share. At the time, TSLA was trading around $450 per share. The odds of TSLA surpassing $1,000 were very slim.

A few weeks later, when the price of TSLA skyrocketed past $800, the price for the contracts increased to almost $100 each, greater than a 33x ROI. Their initial investment of $125,000 became worth $4.3 million. Since they traded in a Roth IRA, their profits were tax free!

Option calls with far out the money strike prices are extremely risky. WSBgod could have easily lost his $125,000, but fortunately they got lucky (or so they claim). They made a good assessment of Tesla's growth potential and it paid off.

I like trading options in my Roth IRA brokerage account. Option trading requires frequent sales and since a Roth IRA is exempt from capital gains or short-term gains taxes, I like the tax advantages. In a regular non-IRA brokerage account, you can reduce your taxes by trading in options that are long-term equity anticipation securities (LEAPS). LEAPS are publicly traded options contracts with expiration dates that are longer than one year in the future. If you hold LEAPS for longer than a year and one day, they are subject to capital gains tax instead of short-term gains tax, which can sometimes be a 15% savings.

I use about 10% to 30% of my Roth IRA to trade options. I'm fairly conservative with my options. Sometimes, I will buy weekly or short-term options if I expect a quick upswing in a stock price. This frequently happens if a news article or short seller publishes a negative report that I disagree with. A popular short seller may publish a report that causes the stock price to gap down temporarily. If I continue to be bullish on the company, I'll use that gap down as an opportunity to load up on more stocks or options. I occasionally play with out the money calls, but usually I prefer calls near the strike price or slightly below.

Once you understand the call option, all the other option strategies become easier to understand. Even the most advanced option strategies are basically a combination of buying and selling different option contracts. There is a plethora of ways to structure options strategies. Buying open call options works best if a stock has a lot of future growth potential, selling call options work if the stock price stays the same or drops, there are other option strategies that make profit during market volatility, and still there are other strategies that make profit during low volatility. Investopedia.com is a great resources to learn more about option trading. The options are endless.

Strategy 4: Technical Analysis

Humans are visual creatures. By some estimates, 90% of our understand of the world is from our sense of vision. The human brain can recognize an image or pattern even if it sees it for brief instant, as little as thirteen thousandth of a second (0.013 s). Investors frequently use technical analysis of charts to make investment decisions because it is easier for our brain to process visual information.

One of the fundamental analysis tools they use are called candlesticks. A candlestick is a bar symbology that allows investors to quickly analyze a stock's performance over a period of time. A candlestick can be for any duration, such as 1 second, 15 minutes, or 24 hours. Whatever time period, a candlestick has five elements: opening price, closing price, max price, minimum price, and color. The color is usually green or white if the price increased between the opening and closing prices, and the color is red or black if the price decreased between opening and closing. Candlesticks provide a quick visualization of a stock's performance.

Candlestick Charts

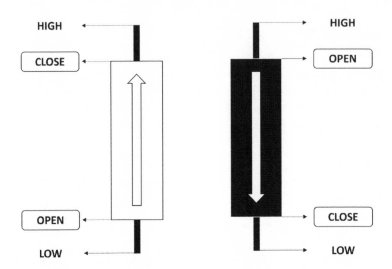

Here is an example of an actual chart for AAPL. This chart is made up of 5-minute candles from opening bell at 9:30 AM to 4:00 pm on February 2, 2021. If you look at the first candle, you can see that the stock opened around $135.75 and sometime within the first five minutes of trading, it peaked for the day around $136.25. After that, the stock fluctuated throughout the day before closing down at around $135. If you are feeling up to a challenge, look at the chart and see if you can identify any patterns.

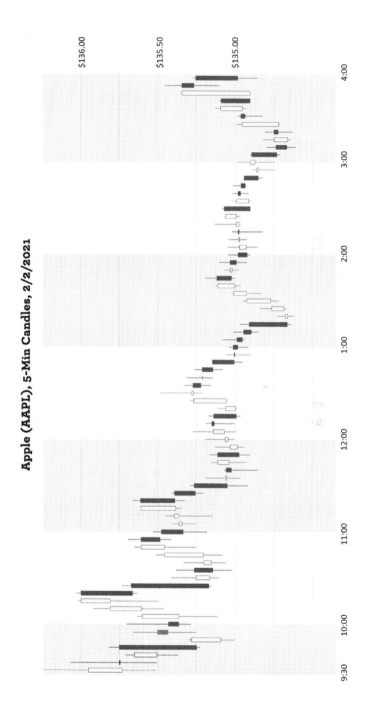

Apple (AAPL), 5-Min Candles, 2/2/2021

One example of a basic pattern is the *three-line strike*. The three-line strike is characterized by three ascending or descending candlesticks followed by a rapid gap down or up in the opposite direction. A similar three-line strike pattern repeats itself at least three times in this single day of AAPL trading. If a savvy investor recognized this pattern developing after three consecutive rising candlesticks, they could open a put option (a bet that the stock price will decline) after the third rising candlestick. Fifteen to thirty minutes later, they could close that option for a profit.

Another pattern is a wedge. In the AAPL example, the three consecutive three line strikes form a wedge which shows the stock price consolidating around $135.25 leading into mid-day. A wedge usually precedes a breakout.

After the consolidation, the stock price breaks lower after about 12:30 and enters a *double bottom* pattern. The double bottom resembles the letter W. In a double bottom, the stock price declines until it bounces off of a support level. It then rises to a resistance level before bouncing off a support level again. This pattern predicts that if the stock breaks through the resistance, it will continue to trend up. In this example, AAPL does break through the resistance level, but only momentarily before descending back down.

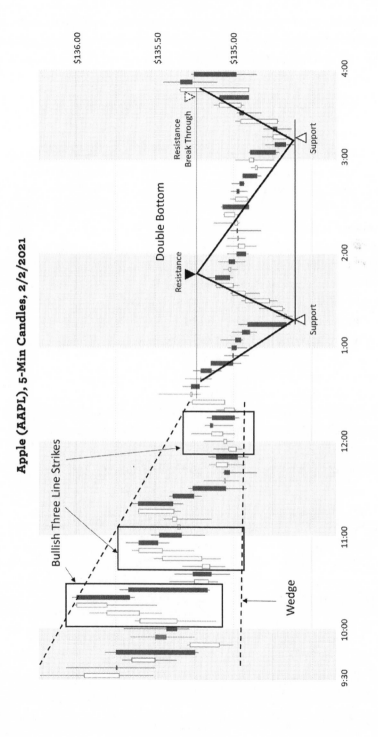

Apple (AAPL), 5-Min Candles, 2/2/2021

Bullish Three Line Strikes

Double Bottom

Resistance
Break Through

Resistance

Support

Support

Wedge

$136.00

$135.50

$135.00

9:30 10:00 11:00 12:00 1:00 2:00 3:00 4:00

There are a plethora of difference candlestick and chart patterns. Some examples include: descending triangles, wedges, pennants, flags, head and shoulders, cup and handles, evening stars, haramis, and Fibonacci retracements. Most day traders use 5 or 15-minute candlesticks, but they could equally be applied to intervals as short as a few seconds or as long as a year. The different types of patterns are endless. Some of these patterns have good prediction capabilities and others not as much.

There are a few challenges to trading using technical chart analysis. The first challenge is that it requires a lot of time to catch great patterns. Most day traders that use technical analysis continuously watch stock charts throughout the day. The most advanced day traders frequently have multiple computer monitors with dozens of windows open, looking for the perfect technical set up. Most active duty service members do not have the free time required to become a skilled day trader.

Another reason why technical analysis is difficult is because of human nature. Humans love patterns. Humans naturally recognize patterns and tend to see patterns in everything, even in places where patterns do not exist. The ability to recognize patterns helps us process information quickly and efficiently. It is a skill set that is vital to our survival.

Here is a pattern. Can you predict what will come next?

Jane tosses a coin seven times. The coin tosses reveal: heads, tails, heads, tails, heads, tails, heads, _____.

Can you guess what the next coin toss will be?

The human brain would naturally guess that the next coin toss will be tails. Or a pessimist may choose heads because they expect the heads-tails pattern to break. Both strategies are flawed.

We know that coin tosses are independent events. A predictive pattern is imaginary. Every coin toss is independent of previous coin tosses and we know that the next coin toss has equal chance of landing heads or tails. In coin tosses, past performance does not predict future success. Although we know this scientifically, our brain still has a hard time ignoring the heads-tails pattern. This example highlights the risk associated with using technical analysis for investing.

As demonstrated with the coin flip, we frequently perceive patterns that do not exist. Furthermore, stock prices, companies, and market behavior are not constrained to follow patterns. In many cases, bullish three line strikes are not followed by a reversal gap down. Instead, they are followed by even more bullish trading upward. There are countless examples of stocks that followed traditional patterns and there are almost as many examples of stocks that dismissed patterns.

Humans are prone to confirmation bias and will place greater emphasis on examples that support their beliefs instead of conducting a non-bias data driven analysis. This is why technical traders must continuously evaluate and refine their strategies. When combined with other strategies, technical analysis and charts can be a great tool to help investors as long as they don't fall victim to irrational bias.

Strategy 5: Algorithmic Trading

When it comes to recognizing patterns in stock behavior, computers are much better at performing non-bias analysis than humans are. Although investors have used computers to program trading algorithms for decades, these algos are becoming more popular due to: 1) increased amounts of available data, 2) decreasing computer costs, and 3) advancements in artificial intelligence. Those algos present a huge challenge for retail investors.

Every candlestick is fundamentally four numbers (opening, closing, high, and low). Humans use candlestick charts because they are easier for us to understand then looking at a table of hundreds of numbers, but computers can process that data easily. A coder with basic skills could create a computer algorithm that automatically recognizes three line strike patterns and executes trades automatically. Not only could these algos recognize candlestick patterns, but they could also be programed to make decisions based upon additional data, like price to earnings ratios, trading volume, time of day, day of the week, or even the stock sentiment on Twitter.

These algo programs have become more and more prevalent over the past decade. They have been known to cause wild price swings. For example, algos caused a flash crash on May 6th, 2010. During the flash crash, a British financial advisor used a spoofing algorithm to manipulate the market. That spoofing algorithm trigged a cascading series of sales by other non-related algorithms. The result was a rapid, widespread market sell off. Within minutes, the Dow Jones dropped 9% and sent the market into a tailspin. Spoofing algorithms are now illegal, but algorithmic trading persists and is even more prevalent now than it was in 2010.

Another example of how algos affect the market occurred in 2020. December 18th was the last day of trading before Tesla joined the S&P 500. The 18th was generally a negative day for TSLA, but in the last 15 minutes of trading, the stock price shot up unexpectedly. In these 15 minutes, it is suspected that algos drove the price of TSLA up from $630 to $670. Even for a popular and volatile stock like TSLA, a 6% increase in a few minutes was unexpected. Algos frequently cause these abnormal stock behaviors.

The problem with these algorithms is that they are making technical analysis more and more difficult for retail investors. If a pattern develops in a stock, algos frequently capitalize on the movement and execute trades long before retail investors know what happened. In the best cases, these algos limit the amount of profit that a retail investor would normally collect. In worst cases, these algos actually anticipate the behavior of retail investors and trade against them, causing retail investors to lose money instead of gaining.

These carnivorous algos are becoming more and more dangerous to retail investors. Instead of trading based upon stock fundamentals, they are instead trading based upon the behavior of retail investors. For example, many retail investors follow popular traders like those in Reddit's Wall Street Bets forum or like @MrZackMorris on Twitter. Increasingly, algos are deployed to monitor these forums. If a stock begins to trend on Wall Street Bets or if @MrZackMorris posts a new stock pick, algos will buy those stocks before retail investors have a chance. Once retail investors begin to move into the position, and drive up the price, the algos will sell as soon as sentiment cools off. Frequently this leaves retail investors holding the bag, at a loss. This is one reason why I increasingly avoid meme stocks.

The good news is that technology is making it easier for retail investors to develop their own algos that can alert traders when a stock matches certain criteria or that can initiate trades automatically. If you are a coder, you can explore GitHub to find plenty of great code repositories that retail investors can use to build their own algos. As a resource, ARK is a very popular ETF management company and they post many of their evaluation models on Github for the public to use.

While it is exciting that a tech savvy investor can build their own algos at home, the bad news is that larger hedge funds are investing hundreds of millions of dollars into building algo super computers that will become more and more sophisticated. Today, large firms are collecting petabytes of data daily and using that information to train machine learning algorithms.

Some people argue that stock trading is rooted in game theory. Well, artificial intelligence algorithms have proven that they can beat humans at every known game—Chess, Jeopardy, Go, Mario Kart, and Rock Paper Scissor are just a few examples. If trading stocks is a game, then it is very probable that more than one hedge funds are already using AI algorithms to win it. For every winner in the stock market, there must be a loser. That loser is usually the retail investor.

I predict that algos will eventually make most types of sound technical analysis impossible for retail investors. Trading platforms are entering the market that make it easier for retail investors to develop their own algorithms, but even these retail algorithms pale in comparison to the big firms that have racks and racks of computers making complex artificial intelligence trades in nanoseconds.

We are in the Golden Age of Retail Investing and artificial intelligence is gradually bringing that age to an end. Fortunately, trading stocks and consistently making a profit is an incredibly difficult task and AI is still a nascent technology. Nonetheless, you should be prepared for the proliferation of artificial intelligence. In my opinion, the best way to beat out AI algorithms is by playing the deep value long game.

AI can predict day to day changes and price swings, but it can't predict broader trends. For example, AI algorithms don't know that artificial intelligence is a growing trend. Nor could they have understood that in early 2020, that the Coronavirus lockdowns in Wuhan China would be a foreboding omen of a larger economic recession. Connecting the dots on larger economic and societal trends and using that information to understand the broader market is currently difficult for AI algorithms but not for the savvy investor who is educated on world trends and geopolitical events.

Gains and Losses

I want to conclude this section on advanced strategies with some comments about gains and losses. I'm going to fast forward for a moment to 2021.

I wrote most of this book in January and February 2021. I had a lot of hubris at the time.

From March 2020 to February 2021, I used strategies like swing trading, leverage, and options to increase the value of my Roth IRA and brokerage accounts from $200,000 to $400,000. I was so confident in my trading skills that I wrote this book about my investment strategies during that time. I doubled my investments in less than a year and I expected to have similar success in 2021. Then reality hit.

In late February, 2021 I checked my Roth IRA and saw a blood bath. Every single one of my positions was negative, many were down by over 10%. My Roth IRA lost $20,000 in a single day.

The loss hurt, but I didn't think much of it. In the afternoon, I invested more into some of my discounted risky tech picks and options.

The next day, the market experienced another blood bath. My Roth IRA was down another $20,000. Worse, was that I had a maintenance call in my other brokerage account. I transferred money into my brokerage account, and doubled down again. Investing more into my favorite tech companies.

Wednesday, the third day was a repeat. Down $20,000 again and another maintenance call. I had a few options contracts that were set to expire in a month or less. Realizing that a short-term rapid recovery was doubtful, I closed many of those options at a loss of 50% or more.

The fourth day, my Roth was down a mere $15,000, but once again, my other account had a maintenance call. On Thursday, I decided that I could not afford to double down any longer. I shifted to a hold strategy and closed out the remainder of my short-term options.

By Friday, the fifth day of the market correction, I had lost over $100,000.

Over the next month, the market continued to decline. By the end of the correction, my portfolio was down almost 40%. I lost most of my gains from the previous year. In less than a month, I lost $150,000—more than an entire year's salary. This experience was a reminder that the fastest way to lose wealth is a concentrated portfolio with leverage.

I realize now that there were market moving events that I did not fully understand. Leading up to February, many investors thought that a market correction was overdue given the ongoing pandemic. Simultaneously volatile trading of GameStop, AMC, and other meme stocks created a lot of instability in the market. Ultimately though, the factor that drove the market correction was something very innocuous—treasury bonds.

Through February, the yield rates of treasury bonds increased steadily. The higher yield rates made the treasury bonds more appealing to institutional investors. As the yield rates increased, institutional investors shifted their investments from high-risk growth stocks to lower risk treasury bonds, resulting in a market correction. I was ignorant of the impact that the treasury market would have on the NASDAQ and I lost a lot of money as a result.

The market is frequently difficult to understand or predict. Even the best investment strategies and the most experienced investors will still lose money on regular occasions. Every investment strategy has risk—some more than others.

When I told my wife, "Babe. This was a bad week for the markets. We lost over $100,000 this week," her response was simple and reassuring, "Don't worry. I know we'll make it back."

LET'S RECAP

Advanced stock market trading strategies can be more profitable than trading common stocks, but each advanced technique has its own unique risk and opportunities.

Stocks frequently swing up or down due to unforeseen and unpredictable events. This is especially true for many advanced investment strategies which have greater volatility.

Many of the advanced trading strategies require a lot of time and energy to conduct due diligence and follow stock performance from day to day. If you choose some of these strategies, like using leverage, option trading, or technical analysis, you need to pay close attention to the market and your investments otherwise you could a loose a lot of money.

Advance investment strategies can be fun and financially rewarding if you understand the risk associated with them.

The fastest way to build wealth is to have a concentrated portfolio with leverage. This is also the fastest way to lose wealth.

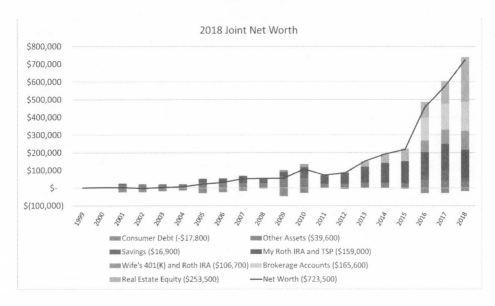

2018 Joint Net Worth

Legend:
- Consumer Debt (-$17,800)
- Other Assets ($39,600)
- Savings ($16,900)
- My Roth IRA and TSP ($159,000)
- Wife's 401(K) and Roth IRA ($106,700)
- Brokerage Accounts ($165,600)
- Real Estate Equity ($253,500)
- Net Worth ($723,500)

CRYPTO

On October 31st, 2008, the mysterious Satoshi Nakamoto published the seminal paper "Bitcoin: A Peer-to-Peer Electronic Cash System." A few months later, on January 9th, 2009, Satoshi released the Bitcoin software and mined the genesis block of bitcoin (block number 0). Embedded in the transaction of this block's digital chain was the text from a U.K. newspaper headline, "Chancellor on brink of second bailout for banks." The rest is history.

When I first heard about bitcoin around 2015, it was trading at $300 a coin. I was intrigued, but not interested enough to invest my money in farfetched science fiction. A year later, it was trading at $600. At that point, I considered buying some bitcoin, but compared to $300, it seemed like bitcoin had become extremely overvalued.

Shortly after that, bitcoin shot up to $10,000 and then $20,000. I felt like a dumbass for not buying it at $600. But then, a few months later, it plummeted back down to about $3,500. I guess I wasn't that dumb after all.

In 2019, it hit $10,000 again. I initially thought, "We've been here before." And then during the pandemic in 2020, it plummeted to $3,000.

A few months later, it was back to $10,000.

In 2020, I finally broke down and bought half a bitcoin when it was $17,000 per coin. Two months later, on Christmas Day 2020, bitcoin broke $25,000, a fitting number for December 25th.

As I write this chapter, less than two months after it broke $25,000, the price of bitcoin is $51,000. I bought more bitcoin as the price increased from $17,000 to $51,000, but I really wish I bought some when it was $600!

Cryptocurrency is fascinating. It is built on a revolutionary technology called blockchain. Every time a cryptocurrency like bitcoin changes from one digital wallet to another, that transaction gets added to that coin's long and ever-growing history which is recorded in that asset's blockchain. Using this digital ledger you can trace the history of every coin, or fraction of coin, from its current holder all the way back to the moment it was created.

The blockchain is secured with strong cryptography software techniques which make hacking cryptocurrencies nearly impossible with current technology. This allows individuals to trade cryptocurrency across the internet without using a third-party like a bank, which normally serves as an insurance party and trusted third agent to transfer money in a process that would otherwise be insecure.

Bitcoin is the grandfather of all cryptocurrencies. It was originally developed for the sole purpose of decentralized digital currency. Today, there are thousands of other cryptocurrencies but most still use blockchain technology similar to Satoshi's original Bitcoin Network. To this day, Bitcoin still has the largest market cap and is the leader of all cryptocurrencies. As of 2021, the total market cap of the cryptocurrency market is about $2 trillion and of this, Bitcoin accounts for about $1.1 trillion of all cryptocurrencies.

Recently, large companies and institutional investors such as PayPal, Square, and Tesla have invested billions of dollars into Bitcoin, and more and more companies are beginning to accept bitcoin as a form of payment.

When discussing this crypto, there is a subtle distinction between the crypto network and the cryptocurrency. The network is a system of software applications and protocols that uses blockchain technology for peer-to-peer transactions. Most networks utilize a digital currency (also called tokens or coins) which facilitates the transactions. Although Bitcoin network (big B) and bitcoin currency (little b) are frequently used interchangeably, it's important to understand that cryptocurrencies involve both a network and a currency. The networks are a central component of each cryptocurrency.

The network includes various aspects such how new coins are digitally mined, the protocols for transferring coins which influence energy consumption, policies for how currencies are upgraded or modified, whether or not the volume of coins in circulations are fixed, and many other aspects. Some networks are rather simple, while others are complex. Regardless, almost every cryptocurrency has different software protocols and governance policies for those protocols. Although the semantics are a minor difference for most conversations, I prefer to reference cryptocurrencies by their network rather than the coin,

Today, there are over 4,000 different cryptocurrencies, each with its own network. Most of these 4,000 currencies are crap and will disappear in a few years, but a few have significant promise. After Bitcoin, Ethereum is the second most significant crypto network in the market today. Ether (ETH) is the digital coin that supports transactions on the Ethereum network (not to be confused with Ethereum Classic (ETC)). Ether currently has a market cap of about $400 billion, about one third of Bitcoin.

Although Bitcoin and Ethereum are frequently discussed in the same conversations, the differences between these two software networks is significant. While Bitcoin was created solely as a digital currency, Ethereum was created to support smart contract functionality. This smart contract functionality allows users to build open-source distributed applications (dapps) and protocols to leverage blockchain technology for a wide range of functions. Here are a few examples of applications that multi-purpose networks like Ethereum support:

With dapps, users can create decentralized financial services (DeFi). These financial products and services support applications like peer-to-peer loan services which can allow anyone to borrow or lend cryptocurrency without going through a trusted third party such as a bank or government.

Non-fungible tokens (NFTs) use blockchain technology to certify unique digital artwork or other digital assets. A new wave of artists are creating digital art and using NFTs to sell ownership of their works.

Although not as sexy as DeFi and NFTs, logisticians can use blockchain networks for supply chain management. A public ledger ensures that distributors know the locations and status of their supplies as they move from factories, through shipping ports, and to consumers.

Dapps and protocols even allow users to create other cryptocurrencies nested within other networks. For example, the Graph Protocol is built on the Ethereum network. Graph allows users to build and publish application programming interfaces to make public information sharable. The Graph token (GRT) is a cryptocurrency that uses unique Ethereum tokens to power the Graph network.

Many crypto enthusiasts believe that the combination of these technologies will usher in a new era of the internet, aka *Web 3.0*, where more power is distributed to individuals instead of large corporations or governments.

It is also important to note that the prices of different coins are not comparable. Although bitcoin cost $50,000 per coin and ether cost $4,000, you should avoid comparing the coins by these prices. You can buy a fractional

0.08 bitcoin and it would initially have the same value in U.S. dollars as 1.00 ether. In other words, ether is not cheaper or a better deal than bitcoin. They are just different.

Many people love Bitcoin or similar networks because they are keenly focused on being a decentralized currency, while other people love multipurpose networks like Ethereum because of the ability to build dapps and protocols. Meanwhile, critics believe that cryptocurrency is a temporary fad that will disappear in a few years. Which camp you fall into will depend a lot on your own beliefs about the future of the world economy.

The benefit of Bitcoin and many other cryptocurrencies is that volume of these available cryptocurrencies is fixed. The total amount of bitcoin in circulation or available to be mined, is limited. No government can ever create more bitcoin. As governments print more fiat currency, the practice will theoretically increase the value of bitcoin, ether, and other coins. Many people, including myself believe that over time, this will decrease the value of the dollar as more paper money enters the market.

While bitcoin, ether, and other cryptocurrencies have not become widely accepted yet as a currency for day-to-day use, the more popular coins have managed to secure their place as a value storage asset, albeit a very volatile one. Similar to gold a decade earlier, people have flocked to bitcoin and other crypto currencies as a hedge against inflation. Similarly, more and more private companies and organizations are beginning to invest in cryptocurrency. It is reported that Amazon, Microsoft, CitiGroup, Anheuser-Busch, and many other companies have invested in Ethereum research. Similarly, organizations like PayPal, Tesla, Square, and even the country of Bulgaria are invested in Bitcoin.

Although the popularity of cryptocurrencies has steadily increased year over year for the past decade, the market still has significant risk for investors. As we've seen in the past, demand can shift in an instant and cryptocurrency prices can drop fast and hard. A big whale could unload a few billion dollars' worth of bitcoin and drive prices down, or conversely a company like Tesla could buy $1.5 billion of bitcoin and drive the price to all-time highs, which contributed to bitcoin's rise in January and February of 2021.

Although there are many risks, I see the greatest risks against cryptocurrency being: 1) hodlers, 2) government regulations, 3) the financial industry, 4) evolving technology, 5) the decentralization paradox, and 6) cybersecurity.

Risk 1: Hodlers

Surprisingly, one of the biggest risks against the success of crypto are the people who are most strongly its advocates. Bitcoin has never really caught on as a currency. Instead of using crypto as a digital currency for peer-to-peer transactions as Satoshi originally intended, its advocates are more likely to be *Hodlers* (a crypto slang for people that hold on for dear life).

99% of Bitcoin transactions are the buying and selling of the asset on currency exchanges and less than 1% is used for peer-to-peer transactions. Most of that 1% is used for illicit black-market transactions and money laundering.

Bitcoin and other cryptocurrencies could become extremely successful if people began using it for peer-to-peer transfers. However, since people think that it will 10x in value, and since the value swings so wildly from day to day, most crypto hodlers refuse to spend any of their crypto. This hodler mentality increases volatility and will decrease the acceptance of crypto.

Risk 2: Government Regulations

Governments rely on their ability to print money and regulate currencies. Since they cannot control crypto currencies, governments may eventually move to restrict its use through regulations and tax codes. Currently, crypto currency is such a small asset class that government has widely ignored it, but if crypto continues its rise, I predict that governments will eventually clamp it down or begin issuing their own crypto currency that they can control. We are already seeing this happen in China.

The U.S. government also taxes cryptocurrency transactions. You create a taxable event whenever you buy, sell, trade, or mine crypto. I overlooked this when I began trading cryptocurrencies. A short time after I began investing in crypto, I tripled my investment. Without thinking, I exchanged most of my bitcoin for ether. As soon as I did that, I created a taxable event on my short-term gains. At the end of the year, I unexpectedly had to pay income tax on the approximately $30,000 in profit. If I was thinking ahead, I could have reduced my tax burden by exchanging crypto currencies when the market was down, or I could have held on to my bitcoin for at least a year to get the capital gains tax rate. The taxes incurred whenever you exchange cryptocurrencies will further encourage hodling and discourages its use as a peer-to-peer currency.

It's also important to note that many cryptocurrency exchanges do not automatically provide their customers tax reporting documents. Many crypto exchanges require customers to utilize a third-party service for tax documents which is an inconvenience and an additional cost.

I should also mention that many crypto exchanges are hosted in foreign countries. If you have a security clearance, you are required to report any foreign holdings, and because many exchanges are hosted in foreign countries, this can include cryptocurrency in some cases. If you have a security clearance, you may need to notify your security office about crypto investments.

Risk 3: The Financial Industry

The financial industry, such as banks and credit card companies, serve as trusted third parties between transactions. Crypto currencies make these functions obsolete. The financial industry worldwide is responsible for about $8 trillion in market capitalization. It is doubtful that they will let cryptocurrency threaten their business models unchallenged. I anticipate that the financial industry will either try to control cryptocurrency markets or influence government to restrict them. Financial service companies will seek to make profit on cryptocurrencies by including it in their list of available services. If they can't make profit on cryptocurrency, then they will do everything they can to disrupt its growth.

An additional risk to cryptocurrencies is that the process of mining and exchanging most cryptocurrencies consumes massive amounts of electricity. Some coins require less energy than others, but bitcoin is one of the larger electrical consumers. In this measure, the financial industry has an advantage. Relative to cryptocurrency, classic money wire exchanges and consumer transactions consume much less energy.

Another advantage that the financial industry has is that the U.S. government federally insures fiat investments in banks, where cryptocurrency is not insured. For this reason, many financial institutions and investors will continue to favor fiat currency over crypto.

Risk 4: Evolving Technology

When I first wrote this section, the top three cryptocurrency networks were Bitcoin, Ethereum, and Litecoin. In the few months it took me to edit and record this book, Litecoin fell from the number three spot and was rapidly overtaken by Cardano. Today, Litecoin is not even in the top ten. It is somewhere around the fifteenth most popular cryptocurrency.

In addition to supply and demand factors, technology evolution and adoption plays an important role in a cryptocurrencies popularity and price. Bitcoin was revolutionary 11 years ago, but today it is actually a legacy technology. Bitcoin is generally considered first-generation technology, while Ethereum and others like it are second generation. Today, new third-generation networks, like Cardano and Solana, are disrupting the market. Many of these new networks have greater technological promise. They have lower electrical energy costs, faster transactions, more secure blockchains, and greater scalability.

In many ways, betting on a crypto coin is like betting on a racehorse. Bitcoin is the leading contender now, followed by Ethereum, but there is always risk that a potential new contender could take over the market in an upset.

Even as I write this book, new contenders like Stellar, Cardano, Solana, and Dogecoin are increasing in popularity. It is not unfathomable to imagine a near future where one of these networks overtakes Bitcoin for the crown.

Risk 5: Decentralization Paradox

Another interesting paradox, especially in regards to Bitcoin, is that the technology was originally created to allow peer-to-peer sharing of decentralized currency. The promise of Bitcoin is that it cannot be controlled. In reality though, about 1,000 people own about 40% of all Bitcoin. These 1,000 investors have the ability to swing the market.

Furthermore, Bitcoin mining operations are relatively centralized. In 2020, five major Chinese mining entities controlled 50% of all mining operations. Later in 2021, China issued a ban on crypto mining which initiated a sell off and drove down the price of Bitcoin from $60,000 to $30,000.

Crypto advocates tout that Bitcoin is decentralized, but in practice a few investors and governments have huge influence over the price of Bitcoin and other cryptocurrencies.

Risk 6: Cybersecurity

There is a story about someone that lost a thumb drive with $220 million worth of bitcoin on it.

Most retail investors do not store their coins on a thumb drive. Instead, they use a marketplace like Binance or Coinbase. Although crypto currencies are difficult to hack, the marketplaces that store them are not so impenetrable. Many smaller marketplaces are notorious for getting hacked. Without the asset being federally insured, it can be impossible to recoup your losses if a hacker steals it from your account. The risk of hacking is greater in crypto marketplaces than in traditional banks. These risks have diminished as crypto exchanges have matured, but the risk is still there.

Customer service on these exchanges is also horrible. If your account does get hacked, or you have issues, good luck getting ahold of a helpful representative on the phone.

Final Thoughts

When it comes to the risks associated with Bitcoin and cryptocurrencies, the last point about cybersecurity deserves a little more attention, not just in terms of cryptocurrency, but in terms of every investment you own.

Although you can't control whether your bank's systems or crypto marketplaces gets hacked, you can take measures to secure your own personal systems.

Two years ago, I had a huge scare. One evening, I was sitting in bed watching TV with my wife when I got a text alert from Wells Fargo, "Your security code for online login is ####. Please do not share."

This was the type of two-factor authentication message I received normally after I tried to login to my bank's website. The problem was that I didn't try to login to the website.

I jumped out of bed. Between my personal and business accounts, I had over $200,000 in my bank account.

I immediately called the bank. They reported that there were no issues with my account. They did not keep records of failed login attempts and could not tell me if someone was trying to get into my account.

The bank could not confirm it, but I suspected that my password was compromised. I had the bank freeze my account until I could implement security measures.

I ran the full suite of antivirus software on my computer—no viruses found—and took some other cybersecurity measures. I changed all my passwords and made sure that all my accounts had multi-factor authentication turned on. Instead of text message authentication, I upgraded to multifactor authentication apps. As always, I made sure that every account used a different password.

I am not completely sure if my password was compromised, and if so, how a hacker would have gotten it. Regardless, I took the risk very seriously.

Cybersecurity is an ever-evolving landscape, and attackers are becoming more and more savvy. It can be difficult and frequently annoying to manage dozens of passwords, multiple authentication forms, and a suite of different antivirus applications. You may feel paranoid inspecting the URLs for every single email or text message before clicking on anything. At times, you may wonder if you are one step away from wearing a tinfoil hat. Yet these measures are necessary to minimize your risk of getting hacked.

Intelligent investors minimize unnecessary risk and cybersecurity is no exception. Implement strong cybersecurity as part of your investment strategies.

With all of the aforementioned risks associated with cryptocurrency, you may wonder why anyone would ever invest in crypto. Many hodlers passionately believe that crypto is the future. They believe that the future decentralization of currency is inevitable and necessary for the future success of our civilization—I'm not sold.

I love blockchain technology and am a big fan of dual-purpose networks like Ethereum, but I'm not the biggest fan of Bitcoin. I own some of both, but mostly because of FOMO.

I don't think that Bitcoin will ever replace fiat currency, but just in case it does, I wouldn't want to miss out. Perhaps my FOMO is exactly what Satoshi Nakamoto predicted when he said, "It might make sense just to get some in case it catches on. If enough people think the same way, that becomes a self-fulfilling prophecy."

LET'S RECAP

There are many cryptocurrencies. Bitcoin is the current leader of cryptocurrencies, while the Ethereum network has a lot of potential to make open-source blockchain technology more popular. There are thousands of other cryptocurrencies that each have their own niche.

There are many risks associated with crypto. Hodler mentality, government regulations, pressure from financial institutions, and evolving technology may limit its adoption,

Cybersecurity is extremely important when it comes to investing. This is especially true with cryptocurrencies which are not federally insured. For any important personal or financial accounts, be sure to use strong passwords, multi-factor authentication apps, and a VPN when using public Wi-Fi.

Cryptocurrency can be a good hedge against inflation and can be a great addition to a diversified investment portfolio.

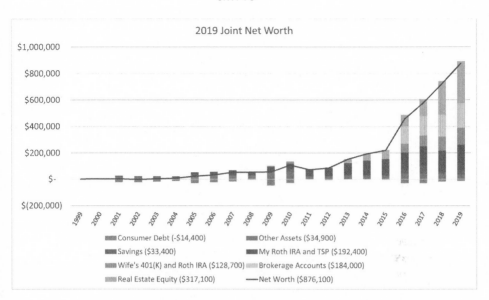

CHILDREN

By some miracle, I've managed to achieve the rank of lieutenant colonel and served in jobs that I loved!

On top of that, I have an amazing family. I met and fell in love with one of the most amazing women in the world. She is funny, intelligent, kindhearted, and fine as hell. Together, we built an incredible life.

Shortly after getting promoted to lieutenant colonel, I experienced another miracle: the birth of our daughter.

Despite my professional successes, my greatest achievement is being a father. My best investment is my family. My wife and precious baby girl bring me happiness and joy every day—the ROI has immeasurable.

When I look back at my life, I can clearly divide it into everything that happened before my daughter's birth, and everything that happened afterwards. The satisfaction that I get from my career or any financial source, cannot compare to the happiness I feel when I see her smile.

But this is a book about financial freedom. Children may elevate your purpose in life, but I must admit that they are expensive. It's no wonder why my old executive officer was so envious of my previous DINK status.

It can be difficult to save money when you have children, and even more difficult if your spouse is a stay-at-home wife or husband. I didn't intend to wait until I was a LTC before having children, but that's what happened. At this point, most of my peers have children in high school, some are sending their children off to college, and I feel like I am well behind them.

I do not tell people when they should or should not have children. I think that whether you have children early in life, or later in life, they always come at the perfect time. However, there are benefits to having children earlier in life. For example, pregnancy and birth is easier when both parents are young, and young parents have more time to enjoy their empty nest golden years later in life. On the flip side, older parents usually are more mature, have established careers, and more financial security. My wife and I fall into the latter category.

Together, my wife and I make close to $300,000 a year and have a net worth of over $1 million. We've done plenty of travelling and enjoyed the DINK life. On the flip side, I'll be raising a teenage girl until I'm 60 years old.

I completely recognize that it is difficult to build wealth as a young parent when a larger percentage of your income goes to supporting your family. This is especially true if you are a single-income family. It is possible to save money if you have children and a stay-at-home spouse but requires a lot of sacrifices. I can't say if waiting to get pregnant is a good or bad decision, but I can say that similar to any other investment, the decision on when or if to have a child will depend on your own personal goals, priorities, and risk factors.

Of course, parents sometimes have children when they don't expect them, and other times parents can't get pregnant when they try their hardest. God has a say in the process as well.

When you do have a children, one of the most common goals of parents, including myself is to help support their children with all things, including finically. You also want to help develop your children into productive members of society that will fulfill their own purpose in life.

Financially, one of the most common vehicles you can use to help your child is a 529 plan. Similar to a Roth IRA or Roth TSP, a 529 plan allows parents to contribute post-tax money into an investment account. Most 529 plans include a handful of mutual fund investment options, like ones that follow the S&P 500.

Unlike IRAs or TSPs, 529 plans are primarily used for educational purposes. Qualified distributions are tax free if used for education related expenses. Each state has their own policies, but generally qualified distributions include items like tuition and fees, books, and special needs services. Although usually geared towards college, qualifying expenses can also include K-12 tuition.

Each account has an account holder and a beneficiary. You can set up a 529 plan at any time, even if you do not have children yet, but most parents wait until after their children are born.

When you set up a 529 plan, the parent is the account holder and the child is the beneficiary. Until the age of majority, the parent controls the account, not the child. After the age of majority the child takes control of the account. Usually, the age of majority is 18 or 21 depending on the state. The max that you can contribute to a 529 varies by state. Depending on the state, the total lifetime contribution limit is $235,000 to $520,000. Most states also have annual contribution limits.

I love investing post-tax money. It is my favorite kind of money. So, after we gave birth to our girl, we opened up a 529 plan. Leading up to the birth, we set aside $25,000. After we got her social security card, we created her 529 and invested $25,000 in it. We plan to continue to contribute a little to it each year, but we hope that compounding interest will turn our $25,000 investment into $100,000 by the time our girl goes to college. Over the next few years, we plan to contribute another $25,000 which should bring her available college fund up to $200,000. By the time she goes to college in 20 years, I expect that most of the top-ranking schools will cost between $50,000 to $100,000 per year. If she does not use her savings for undergrad, she can use it for her master's degree or PhD. In a separate book, we can argue about how ridiculously and unnecessarily expensive college is!

Additionally, I also have half of my Post 9/11 G.I. Bill available. Currently, the Post 9/11 G.I. Bill covers:

Tuition and fees. The current rate for a private university is $25,162 per year, but I expect that to change over the next 18 years.

A monthly housing allowance equivalent to the E-5 basic housing allowance (BAH) for the school's local area.

Up to $1,000 per year for books and supplies.

The G.I. Bill is good for a total of 36 months, which is about four academic years. I already used half of this to pursue my own PhD in my free time while I was on active duty.

Currently, the requirements for transferring the G.I. Bill benefits to a dependent is that a service member must have served at least 6 years. When you transfer benefits, you also incur a 4-year service obligation which runs concurrently to other service obligations. These rules change periodically, so do your own research on VA.gov as required.

We didn't give birth to our daughter until my 17th year of my service, three years before I planned to retire. In order to retain the ability to transfer the benefit in the future, I transferred the benefits to my wife before my 16th year of service. Later, I will transfer the benefits to our daughter without incurring an additional service obligation.

The Post 9/11 G.I. Bill is an amazing benefit to military members if you qualify for it. Between the G.I. Bill and our 529 plans, I expect that our daughter will be able to go to college without incurring any student debt and without us paying out of pocket. Of course, I secretly hope that she will go to West Point and be the First Captain.

Now, here is where it gets really interesting. If our girl does go to West Point (free for us), then we could withdraw the 529 plan money ourselves and keep it as long as our girl has not reached the age of majority. We would incur a 10% penalty and need to pay required taxes.

Or we could change the beneficiary and save it for our grandchildren. Another three decades of compounding interest could turn our initial $50,000 investment into $1.6 million or more. I'd be an immensely proud 90-year-old grandparent if I could give my grandchildren $1.6 million. I'm ok with my grandchildren being trust fund babies. That's much more than the $2,000 my grandmother left me when she passed away!

Giving our children and grandchildren money is great, but the more important goal for us as parents is to teach our daughter how to make money for herself. We want her to learn that money is a product of delivering value to the world. We want to instill in her a spirit of hard work, intelligent work, and duty to her community and society. This can be extremely hard to do when your parents make $300,000 per year, you have college paid for, and you have a nanny, house cleaner, and a landscaper—all luxuries that neither my wife nor I had as children.

Some parents in our position take an approach that their children should suffer like we did. They make their children mow the grass, scrub the toilets, or walk ten miles to school to learn the value of adversity. There is truth that suffering can build character. Growing up in a lower income community certainly worked out well for me and my wife, but I'm not sure that we could replicate the same experience for our children.

Our goal is not to make our daughter suffer like we did. I plan to teach her how to mow the grass once or twice, so that they learn the skill, but I don't plan to fire our landscaper anytime soon. Instead, we will need to teach her the value of hard work a different way. Additionally, we want to teach her how to help people, how to solve problems for herself, and how to delay temporary gratification in order to achieve later success.

Our baby girl is still a toddler. We still have a long way to go as parents, and I'm learning as I go. Our daughter just recently learned how to walk, so I have not been able to implement any advanced parenting techniques, but here are some parenting ideas that I learned from other well-to-do friends:

Give your kids an allowance, but don't tie it to chores. A small allowance is a great way for children to learn how to manage their own money. If you make the mistake of making them 'earn' their allowance by doing chores, then they will develop a 'what's in it for me' attitude. Children should learn to do chores because they are part of the family team and not because of a reward.

Encourage your children to be entrepreneurs by helping them build a lemonade stand, lawnmower, or some other neighborhood business. Use it as an opportunity to teach them about income and expenses, marketing, and sales.

For Christmas, keep it simple. Refrain from buying dozens of gifts because it makes you, the parent, happy. Children will be happy with a few, thoughtful gifts. The best gifts should come from Mommy and Daddy, not Santa Clause. Let Santa Clause bring the boring gifts, like sweaters or socks, while you give the awesome gifts like the PlayStation 7. Reinforce that, "Mommy and Daddy worked hard so that we could give you these gifts, because we love you so much." Also, get rid of the Elf on the Shelf. Don't train your children to live in a surveillance state.

When your children behave well, reward them with experiences. For example, if your daughter does something nice for a friend, reward her by taking her to get a pedicure or take her to a baseball game. As much as you can, make rewards a surprise and not expected.

Don't reward children that get 'A's on report cards. Nor should you punish children that get 'D's. Instead, reward self-awareness. If a child gets an A, ask them to explain what they did well to earn that grade. Likewise, if a child gets a D, ask them to explain what they could have done better. If they can fully understand their own behavior, and make plans to improve, then reward them.

If you own a small business, put your child to work as soon as possible. Even a toddler can help with small tasks like taking the trash out of our home office, opening up the mail, and picking up papers from the printer. They are really minor tasks, but they emphasis the importance of work and also the rewards that work provides—like vacations, toys, and your family's home. Family businesses are exempt from most child labor laws, and if you own a business, you can legally pay your children reasonable pay for their work beginning at a young age.

As soon as your child begins to work and earn taxable income, whether through a lemonade stand, home business, or summer job at RadioShack, help them open up a Roth IRA. Although IRAs are typically used for retirement, you can also make penalty free withdrawals for qualified education expenses. In some ways, a Roth IRA has more flexibility than a 529 plan which is generally only available for education expenses. Opening an IRA at a young age allows your children to start saving for retirement and college early in life. Compounding interest needs time to work. Imagine how powerful that compounding interest will be if your children begin investing in mutual funds and learning about stocks at five-year-old. That's pure fucking magic.

Our daughter is barely learning how to walk, so we have not been able to implement these strategies yet, but we hope to start soon. I've done professionally and financially well in my life, and I hope that my children can continue to do the same. I hope that I can build wealth not only for myself, but also for future generations of my family.

There are some Scrooges that would be happy to spend every penny they earned in their life. These are the people that say things like, "I want the last check I write to bounce," or "You can't take it with you."

In my opinion, this perspective is incredibly shortsighted. Similar to how I want America to be a great nation long after I pass away, I also want my family to be successful for centuries to come. I want my family to be like the Carnegies and Rockefellers. I want my family to make the world a better place by being founding members of museums, schools, charities, and other benevolent activities. I want my family to make the world a better place by building businesses, discovering the cure for cancer, being amazing artists, or building space stations on Mars. Most importantly, I want my children and grandchildren to live life as their true-self and be able to pursue any productive activity that helps our civilization move forward and makes the world a better place without the same financial and mindset constraints that I had as a child. My goal for financial freedom extends much farther than my own lifetime.

LET'S RECAP

A 529 plan is a tax-advantaged investment vehicle that can help your children pay for qualified higher education expenses. Contributions are made with after-tax money. Investments grow tax free, and withdrawals are tax exempt as long as they are for qualified expense.

The Post 9/11 G.I. Bill is an educational benefit for qualified service members. The benefits include tuition for up to 36 months, a housing allowance, and stipend.

A child can work in a family-owned sole proprietorship business from any age. If a child earns taxable income, they can also contribute to a Roth IRA. In addition to retirement income, a Roth IRA can also be used for qualified education expenses including tuition, fees, books, and room and board.

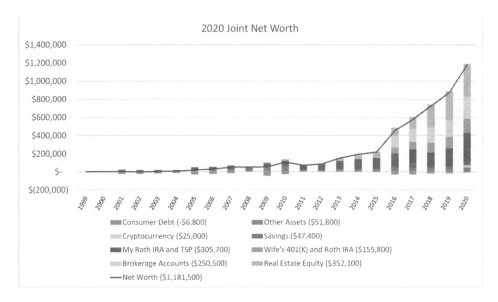

RETIREMENT

"I think we need to plan for worse case," I told my wife as I stood with a marker in hand at the dry erase board in our home office. It was March 2020.

She sat at the small conference room table in front of the board.

"Ok," she said with a stoic face.

I drew two columns on the board.

"Let's start with the most dangerous course of action," I was following the military decision making process I learned in the Captains Career Course, "What do we think is the worst that can happen?"

"I don't know. My clients fire me?"

"Ok," I said as I wrote 'clients fire.'

I inquired further, "I don' think they will all fire you. What percentage do you think would fire you?"

"Um... let's say fifty percent?" she replied uncertainly.

"Ok, fifty percent," as I wrote the number on the board, "How much income would you lose?"

"Let's see. I'd still need to pay Cherie, but I could probably fire Jenny and cancel the marketing contract." She did the math. "Probably sixty-five K."

I wrote '$65,000' on the board. We continued the exercise listed potential outcomes. When we were finished, the board looked like this.

Most Likely	*Most Dangerous*
20% of clients fire us	*50% of clients fire us*
Income down $20,000	*Income down $65,000*
Revenue down $75,000	*Revenue down $150,000*
1x coaches gets sick	*2x staff get sick*
Marketing redux 50%	*1x staff cut*
Day care closed for 3 months	*Marketing company fired*
	Day care closed for 6 months
	We get COVID

In 2019, my wife quite her medical sales job to launch her own sales coaching business. At first, the business was slow and she barely made any money. Eventually she got a few clients.

She used her profits to reinvested back into the business. She hired teams of contractors to build out the website, launch digital sales funnels, and manage social media marketing campaigns. She also travelled to a lot to different conferences to establish herself as a leader in the field of sales and marketing.

At first her expenses were much greater than her income. Fortunately, we prepared for the transition and saved up about $40,000 leading up to the business' launch. She prepared to invest $25,000 to get the business started, and the other $15,000 was to cover living expenses while the business grew.

The transition was somewhat seamless financially. Towards the end of 2019 the business started to pick up steam. She managed to get more clients and had to hire an assistant and three coaches to help her. Soon, her biggest challenge was not in finding new clients, but instead her challenge was finding coaches to work for her.

Less than a year after starting the business, she began paying herself a decent salary of $8,000 per month. It wasn't nearly as much as she was making in medical sales, but the business was taking off. It seemed like quitting her job was a good move... until the coronavirus pandemic began.

Just as the business was picking up steam, coronavirus attacked America and the world. Schools and day care were shut down, we barricaded ourselves in our house, toilet paper was more valuable than gold, and every day we watched Governor Cuomo to get updates on the rising death rates. It was a time of fear and paranoia, not just for us, but for the entire nation.

It seemed like the entire economy was collapsing except for one area, medical sales!

Her old friends in medical sales were making a killing—er, maybe that's a bad description—they were having a very profitable year. Ventilator sales were just the tip of the iceberg. Sales representatives that previously sold X-Ray machines were now selling N95 masks, PPE, and everything else you could imagine that was required in an ICU.

If she stayed in medical sales, we estimate that she could have made $300,000 to $400,000. Instead, she was struggling to grow an infant business.

When she was in medical sales before COVID, she was making about $150,000 a year. Less than a year after starting her business she was making $90,000 per year—not as good as her previous job, but still pretty good.

Now, due to the virus, we were preparing for a most dangerous scenario that would see her income reduce to $25,000, less than minimum wage. We feared that leaving the medical sales job was a huge mistake.

At the same time, I was mentally preparing for retirement. I felt a similar fear growing inside of me. I repeatedly imagined that I would retire and then be unable to get a job, or even worse, be forced to take a job that makes me unhappy. I told myself that I would retire at exactly 20 years of service, but the closer I got to that date, the less certain I was. I considered postponing my retirement for a few years until the market fully recovered from the pandemic. As with most financial decisions, I had to evaluate the risk and opportunities of transitioning to a civilian job during the pandemic.

I'm grandfathered into the old retirement system. As long as I don't fuck up over the next few months, I'll be able to retire and start collecting my pension soon after terminal leave. At a minimum, I should collect half of my high three. As a LTC for the last three years of my career, I'll collect half of the average of my base salary over those three years. It comes out to about $57,000 per year. If I receive disability benefits, I may be able to get more than that.

Disability benefits are complicated, but the key point to remember is that most soldiers who retire after 20 years have some type of service-related disability. For example, I tore my ACL while playing Ultimate Frisbee during the Captain's Career Course, I started to get kidney stones during my second deployment, I have persistent back issues from wearing 40 pounds of body in a vibrating helicopter for years, and now my eyesight is starting to go because I stare at PowerPoints and spreadsheets all day.

None of my health issues are particularly debilitating, but my military service has accelerated my body's deterioration. I am currently in my retirement process, and I spend a large portion of my last year in service going to doctors' appointments to ensure that all of my health issues are properly documented. The VA will review my file and assign me a certain disability percentage. I'm expecting somewhere from 20% to 55%.

When it comes to retirement pay and disability ratings, the math is complicated, but I'll try to explain it simply. If you have 0% disability, then 100% of your retirement pay is taxable.

If your disability is between 1% to 49%, then a percentage of your retirement pay will be tax free. The more disability you have, the more is tax free. Up to 49%, the total amount of your retirement pay remains the same, it's just that the portion of taxable and tax-free income that changes.

If you have a disability rating of 50% or more, then you will receive your standard taxable retirement pay, 50% of your high three, and then you will receive an additional payment from the VA. Theoretically, if you are 100% disabled, you can receive a pension and disability that is nearly equal to your pre-retirement income.

Even if you have a medical history when you retire, but not a disability percentage for it, you need to document it because if it becomes an issue in the future you can seek aid from the Department of Veterans Affairs.

Without going into too much detail about the process, here are two key takeaways. The first is that you need to document all health issues throughout your career. If you have an injury or medical ailment, go to sick call and get it documented. That documentation is an important record of documenting your service-related disabilities. Even if you are deployed and unable to see a doctor, document your medical issues in a logbook and get a doctor to add it to your record as soon as you can. Ensure that you keep records for yourself too.

The second key point to remember is that before you plan to retire, do your own research and talk to people that have been through the process. There are plenty of resources on the internet to help guide you through the retirement process. Sometimes, you may not even know that one of your medical issues qualifies you for disability. Migraines, back aches, plantar fasciitis, these are all minor issues that may qualify you for a percentage of disability.

When it comes to pension, I'm lucky. I am grandfathered into the legacy retirement system. But a few years ago, the department changed their retirement program. In 2018, they fully rolled out the new Blended Retirement System.

The grandfather retirement system allowed for service members to retire at 20 years with 50% of their high three. The new plan decreases that amount to

40%, but unlike the all or nothing grandfather system, the new plan has options available for service members who retire before 20 years. Additionally, the new system introduced TSP matching. The military automatically contributes 1% to all service members TSP regardless of the service members contributions, and after two years of service, the military will match up to 5% of the service members' base pay. The new retirement system also includes a mid-career incentive pay and different options for lump sum payments upon retirement.

The Blended Retirement System is certainly complex. It is not perfect, but the key aspect of it that I like is that it offers service members different options. It also encourages service members to take a more active role in their financial planning. The people who benefit most from the new blended retirement system will be the ones who begin taking full advantage of TSP matching early in their career. This is yet another reason why I recommend that service members begin their career by investing at least 5% into the TSP and gradually increase that amount throughout their career.

The old retirement system worked out well for me because I didn't start saving in my TSP consistently until later in my career, but young officers who begin saving early can game the system to their benefit.

For life beyond the Army, I am extremely lucky that I switched to a functional area instead of staying in my basic operational branch. I'm targeting a job with a salary of $150,000 to $250,000.

My master's degree and the functional area expertise make me incredibly competitive for civilian employment, especially with the major defense contractors. In contrast, most of my peers who stayed in Infantry, Field Artillery, or the other basic branches and then retire as a LTC average starting salaries of $100,000 to $150,000. Although the leadership skills they gained are invaluable, most of the commercial industry does not value leadership the same way the Army does. I've observed that the commercial sector pays greater salaries to vets with experience in operational research, software management, program management, contracting, or business administration. Functional areas like FA26 (Information Network Engineering), FA49 (Operations Research and Systems Analysis), and FA51 (Acquisition Corps), are particular skillsets that are in high demand in the commercial industry.

Most officers transition to functional areas through the Voluntary Transfer Incentive Program. Although each branch and functional area is slightly different, this transition usually happens after completing Company Command. If selected for a functional area, most include some type of transition course, and many functional areas also have funding for graduate school through the Advanced Civil Schooling program.

I always recommend for officers to follow their passions, whether that be Infantry, Special Forces, or functional areas. If you love your operational branch, you should stay operations and be all that you can be. However, if you are looking to broaden your professional skillset and contribute to the national defense in a different kind of way, functional areas are exceptional career choices in my humble and biased opinion.

Since operational leadership experience is not the most sought-after skill, many officers leave the military and go to grad school. With a proper mentor, most officers can get accepted to Ivy League MBA program like Yale, Harvard, or Columbia. Many officers can go to those schools with full scholarships too. My golfing bro that went to Harvard has helped at least ten West Pointers get full rides to his second alma mater.

Regardless of your path after the Army, your West Point network is a huge strength that you should leverage for mentorship, job opportunities, or schools. I estimate that the West Point network is a 20% multiplier. If you are applying for jobs, the West Point connection can help you land one with 20% higher pay; if you are applying to law school, the West Point connection can help you get into a school that's ranked 20% higher; if you're running for congress, the West Point connection can help you get 20% more votes; if you're writing a book, the West Point connection can help you have 20% more sales—hint, hint—you should recommend this book to your classmates.

For these reasons, it is incredibly important to nurture these relationships throughout your time at West Point, while in the Army, and afterwards. Take golf trips with your West Point buddies, join the local AOG chapter whenever you move to a new city, and stay in touch with your professors, sponsors, and TACs. You will be surprised by how many of these peers and senior officers will become generals, CEOs, and Congressmen. Investments in your network also have compounding interest.

As my wife expanded her coaching business, I shared the news with my West Point network and we eventually hired a West Pointers as her partial-CFO and another West Pointer as one of her coaches. Whenever they meet on Zoom, I love to shout "Beat Navy!" It frustrates the hell out of my wife, but we get a big kick out of it.

When the pandemic started, we were prepared for the worse. Instead of my wife making $85,000 a year, we prepared for her to make $25,000. We expected that the looming recession would cut the number of her clients in half and we were preparing for worst case scenarios of our family getting sick too.

During the height of the pandemic, I was also beginning to plan my exit strategy from the military. I had a huge amount of uncertainty in what kind of company I wanted to work for, how much salary and benefits I could get, and where we wanted to live after the military. I could probably write an entire book about this process, but since I am still going through it at the time of writing this first book, I'll save it for a sequel.

The pandemic did not hurt my wife's business as bad as we expected. Half of her teammates did get sick during COVID, but all of them recovered well. My wife, baby, and myself also got COVID, but fortunately we got it after my wife and I were vaccinated. We also recovered well. That was the worse that happened. She didn't have to fire anyone.

Although new client hires slowed down temporarily in March through May, by August the business surged to new highs. It turns out that a lot of business owners needed a lot of coaching during COVID. The pandemic turned their worlds upside down and my wife and her company helped them make sense of it all. They helped companies transition to virtual offices, showed them how to navigate small business loans and payroll protection programs, and modernized their clients' sales processes to new digital tools and social media. Although I don't use it, my wife was at the forefront of adopting Tik Tok for business.

I'm utterly impressed with how many small business owners my wife and her team were able to help during this exceedingly difficult time. I've found that the businesses that struggled most were the ones that were stuck in their old ways and consistently tried to return to normal. While the businesses that succeeded the most were the ones who adapted to their environment and accepted that the COVID environment is the new normal. Seeing my wife and her clients succeed has given me hope in the American economy and also hope in myself.

I know that many families were suffering in 2020 due to unemployment, illness, and loss of loved ones. And I also know that many families are continuing to suffer through 2021. Those families have my sincere sympathy. I never take for granted how fortunate and blessed my family has been. I hope that our nation can fully recover from this pandemic quickly.

Although 2020 and 2021 were stressful and challenging years, I learned that you must not let fear paralyze you. I am still anxious about retirement, but I know that as long as I am flexible, eager to learn, and can adapt to my new environment, then I will be ok.

Wherever I end up after I retire, I know that life will be different than my time in the Army. I will definitely miss the comradery, sense of duty, and mission focus, but I know that I need to eventually say goodbye to the uniform to open up new opportunities in my life. I am eagerly and anxiously looking forward to the transition to civilian life.

LET'S RECAP

To take full advantage of the new Blended Retirement System, officers should begin their career by contributing at least 5% to their TSP so that they can get contribution matching as soon as it is available.

Throughout your career, it is important to properly document any medical issues, injuries, or ailments. These records will be important to determine disability benefits when you retire.

Functional areas offer a great opportunity to broaden your professional skillset beyond your basic branch, which can help you if you transition to a civilian career.

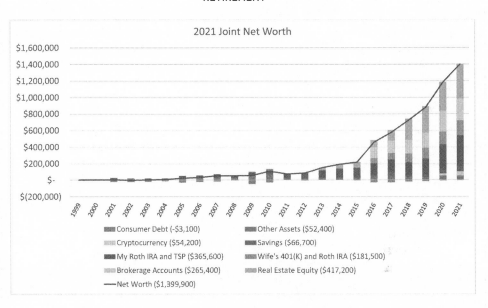

2021 - 2022

RETREAT

I remember a conversation I had with my father a few years ago.

"This is unbelievable," my dad said to me at my promotion ceremony, "Look at that. The Constitution, right there. I can't believe this."

My dad and I had this conversation in 2018 at my promotion ceremony to LTC. As an officer in the Armed Forces, we have the ability to get promoted at the National Archives Museum in Washington, D.C. In a small intimate ceremony, I got promoted from major to lieutenant colonel at the museum within arm's reach of the original U.S. Constitution.

Throughout my years at West Point and military career, I've raised my hand many times and recited:

> I _____, do solemnly swear that I will support and defend the
> Constitution of the United States against all enemies, foreign and
> domestic; that I will bear true faith and allegiance to the same; that I
> take this obligation freely, without any mental reservation or purpose of
> evasion; and that I will well and faithfully discharge the duties of the office
> on which I am about to enter. So, help me God.

It was utterly amazing to have my final promotion ceremony in front of the sacred document that I swore an oath to protect. My dad was right, it was unbelievable.

Perhaps "unbelievable" is the story of my life. In junior high school, when I was a young hoodlum, I used to hang out with the local drug dealers and gangs at the local basketball courts. Fortunately, my dad caught me one day and straightened me out.

A few years later, by some miracle and with the help of a West Point minority outreach admissions officer, I got accepted to attend West Point.

At West Point, I was a mediocre student at best. I believed in the mantra "2.0 and go." I put average effort into studying, and believed that sports, trip sections, girls, and weekend passes were much more rewarding than a Gold Star Wreath. As such, I really enjoyed my time at West Point (except for the time I got demoted and had to walk area tours). Despite my brief disciplinary troubles, I got to experience amazing things like the Forbes super yacht, beating Navy in football our bicentennial year, and building friendships with my classmates from all over the world.

I finished with a 2.7 GPA which put me around the middle of class ranking. I listed Aviation as my first choice, but honestly thought I was going to get Infantry instead. Well, I surprised myself when I branched Aviation and got to spend the first eight years of my career flying helicopters—how cool is that!

I flew incredible missions all over the world. I've flown down Panama City Beach, over the Great Lakes, across the dunes in Iraq, in the mountains of Afghanistan, and I even flew past the Statue of Liberty!

Then the Army sent a dumb cavalry scout like me to graduate school, for free, and afterwards invested hundreds of thousands of dollars in training me with incredible professional skills.

I've worked with America's finest military members, public servants, and industrial partners. I've built friendships and professional relationships that have made life incredibly more rewarding.

Along the way, I made a bunch of stupid financial decisions, but a few smart ones too. As if by magic, I've saved hundreds of thousands of dollars and increased my net worth to well over one million. Ever since I bought my first stock as a Yuck, I've been on a continuous growth path, learning more and more about finances and also about myself.

The best part of all is that I've got to do all of this while serving my country, the great United States of America. For twenty years, when duty called, I answered eagerly. Whether I was providing air cover to convoys in Iraq, helping an enlisted soldier go to flight school, or explaining the importance of big data to a congressional staffer, my career has been full of exciting and rewarding experiences.

Throughout my career, I've always given my best at every job. Although I think I've always kicked ass, my superiors have rarely seen it the same way. I've had a consistent record of mediocre officer evaluation reports. I've never been promoted early, but I've never been passed over either. Instead, I always fell in the middle of the pack. Yet, consistency has seemed to pay off and to my surprise I got promoted to lieutenant colonel.

When it comes to investing, I've made many mistakes. I've lost money when I chased risky investments because I wanted a quick profit. I've also lost money when I traded emotionally instead of with sound investment principles. I ignored my TSP for years and wasted most of my deployment money on a motorcycle and fancy vacations. At times, I partied way too hard instead of saving money for a rainy day. I had a major financial set back when I got divorced and even greater setbacks when I missed critical market indicators. I've experienced the pain of losing $100,000 in a single week and I know that it can happen again. I am not the ideal role model of a cadet, officer, or investor. Yet, I've had some successes that I am proud of—financially, professionally, and personally.

I've known many officers and soldiers who contemplate leaving the Army so that they can make more money as a civilian. There is certainly truth that many civilian jobs pay more than the Army, especially given some of the unique skill sets that we have. However, I know many retired officers who would have been more financially successful if they stayed in the Army.

I hope this book has shown, that it is possible to serve in the military service honorably and be very financially successful at the same time. Financial security is a key element that has allowed me to spend time with my family, pursue the jobs that I love, and lead in the ways that I think are most impactful.

This is a book about finances, but there is much more to life than just financial success. For me, my family, duty to my country, and being a leader in my community are much more important than making money. If I can succeed in those areas, then I can proudly say, "Well done!"

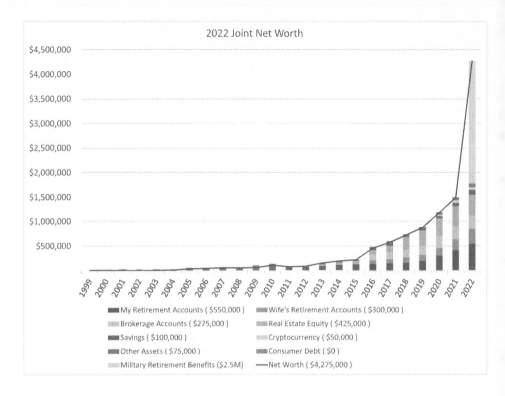

2022 Joint Net Worth

Legend:
- My Retirement Accounts ($550,000)
- Wife's Retirement Accounts ($300,000)
- Brokerage Accounts ($275,000)
- Real Estate Equity ($425,000)
- Savings ($100,000)
- Cryptocurrency ($50,000)
- Other Assets ($75,000)
- Consumer Debt ($0)
- Military Retirement Benefits ($2.5M)
- Net Worth ($4,275,000)

THANK YOU

Thank you for reading *Black & Gold*. I hope that you found it helpful or inspiring. If you have any questions or just want to say hello, I'd love to connect with you on Facebook or Twitter. Please connect with me **@TheCadetX**.

If something in this book was useful, could you help me out?

Would you <u>please</u> leave a 5-star review on Amazon.

I'm an independent, self-published author. I write in my free time. I don't have a marketing team, expensive editor, publisher, or time to go on book tours. The only way I market this book is by word of mouth. Your referrals and Amazon reviews are a tremendous help in spreading the word about this book. With your support, we can help future generations of cadets and officers improve their financial literacy.

To show support, please leave a 5-star review on Amazon and share this book with your friends on social media—THANK YOU!

Go Army!
Beat Navy!